Don't Waste
Your Sorrows

Don't Waste Your Sorrows

Paul E. Billheimer

A Sequel to
DESTINED FOR THE THRONE

A New Look at

the Age-old Question:
WHY DO THE RIGHTEOUS SUFFER?

CHRISTIAN LITERATURE CRUSADE
Fort Washington, Pennsylvania 19034

CHRISTIAN LITERATURE CRUSADE
Fort Washington, Pennsylvania 19034

CANADA
1757 Avenue Road, Toronto, Ontario M5M 3Y8

GREAT BRITAIN
The Dean, Alresford, Hampshire

AUSTRALIA
P.O. Box 91, Pennant Hills, N.S.W. 2120

Printed in the United States of America

DEDICATED
TO ALL SUFFERING SAINTS

My loving appreciation to

My Wife

who has labored "more abundantly" and at
great cost in assisting with the development
and preparation of the manuscript for this
volume.

During the fifty-seven years of our marriage the Lord has
used us to teach one another agape love. He continues to
bring us into an increasing oneness in Himself which
satisfies the deepest heart longings.

My Thanks To
Mr. David Monroe for his valuable assistance in reproducing the manuscript for
publication.

APOLOGIA

I am not writing about love because I feel qualified. Far from it. On the contrary, I wish to take this opportunity to confess, with penitential sorrow, to my wife, my children, my relatives and friends, to any of our erstwhile parishioners, to former school faculty, staff, students, and beloved radio audience into whose hands this book may come, that I have been utterly at fault in this matter of love. God has dealt with me very sorely during many years of severe discipline, heart-searching, and chastening, to show me the truths set forth in this volume.

Although it has been agonizingly painful, I would not have missed it at any conceivable cost. My gratitude to God for His faithfulness and patience with me knows no bounds.

The greatest regret I have is that I have been so slow a learner. My greatest joy is that God did not give me up.

Paul E. Billheimer

PREFACE

This book is designed as a sequel to *Destined for the Throne*, and is based upon the same cosmology. The term "cosmology" means the principles under which the universe is operated. This cosmology holds that the ultimate goal of the universe is the Church (Rom. 8:28 and Eph. 3:9-11).

It affirms that the universe, including this planet, was created to provide a suitable habitation for the human race. The human race was created in the image and likeness of God to provide an Eternal Companion for the Son. After the fall and the promise of redemption, the Messianic race was born and nurtured to bring in the Messiah. The Messiah came for one intent and only one: to give birth to His Church, thus to obtain His Bride.

This cosmology asserts that, as far as Scripture reveals, all that God has done from all eternity, and all that He will do until the Marriage Supper of the Lamb, is concerned primarily with one thing, and only one: the gathering out and training of His Bride for her exalted position of co-rulership with the Son over His vast, ever-expanding, eternal kingdom in the ages to come. *All that precedes the Marriage Supper of the Lamb from all eternity is only preliminary to God's eternal enterprise.* Only after the

Bride is on the throne with her Lover and Lord will God be ready to unveil His creative program for the eternal ages.

In *Destined for the Throne* it is claimed that God ordained the system of prayer not primarily as a way of getting things done (He is entirely self-sufficient), but as "on-the-job" training for the Bride-elect in overcoming the forces hostile to God as a part of her preparation for the throne. *Overcoming is a prerequisite to enthronement* (Rev. 3:21). God ordained the plan of prayer as an apprenticeship in which the Bride-elect is learning "the trick of the tools," how to use the weapons of *prayer and faith* in triumphing over evil, as a preparation for her queenly role.

This present volume considers SUFFERING, in addition to PRAYER, as another aspect of the Bride-elect's training for sovereignty. If we overcome, we shall reign (Rev. 3:21). "If we suffer, we shall also reign" (2 Tim. 2:12). God designed the system of prayer to equip or qualify her with the techniques, the skills, and the "know-how" for rulership. He has further designed that SUFFERING, which is a consequence of the Fall, shall produce the CHARACTER and DISPOSITION, the compassionate spirit which will be required for rulership in a government where THE LAW OF LOVE IS SUPREME.

In Ephesians 1:9-10 we learn that in the future social order toward which the universe is moving (otherwise called the kingdom of God), God plans to bring together under one Head all things, the entire universe, with all of its principalities and powers, the entire hierarchy of authorities and rulers, the total population of personalities, both in heaven and on earth and "under the earth" (Phil. 2:10). "Having made known unto us the mystery of his will, according to his good pleasure which he hath purposed in himself: that in the dispensation of the fulness of times he might gather together in one all things in Christ, both which are in heaven, and which are on earth; even in him.'' There can be no unity without love. All discord, division, and fragmentation is the result of deficiency in love. Therefore, in a perfectly unified universe THE LAW OF LOVE IS SUPREME.

When one is born again he immediately enters apprenticeship in training for rulership. Since *agape* love* is an essential qualification for the exercise of authority in the heavenly social order, this apprenticeship is for the development of this love.

Because tribulation is necessary for the decentralization of self and the development of deep dimensions of agape *love, this love can be developed only in the school of suffering.* It grows and develops only by exercise and testing. This may explain the relationship between sainthood and suffering by showing *WHY there is no sainthood without suffering.* It may also show why the greatest saints are often the greatest sufferers. It is an attempt to answer the age-old question: "*Why* do the righteous suffer?''

To summarize: All born-again people are in training for rulership. Since the supreme law of that future social order, called the kingdom of God, is *agape* love, therefore their apprenticeship and training is for the learning of deep dimensions of this love. But deep dimensions of this love are learned only in the school of suffering. Even after the new birth and the filling with the Holy Spirit, which are only beginning experiences, greater dimensions of this love are developed only by exercise and testing. Purity is one thing and maturity is another. The latter comes only

---

Agape love is the love which loves because of its own inherent nature, not because of the excellence or worth of its object. According to the Bible dictionary it is spontaneous, automatic love.

through years of suffering. "If we suffer, we shall also reign" — because where there is little suffering, there is little love; no suffering, no love; no love, no rulership.

CONTENTS

Redeemed ☆ The Only Valid Explanation of the Universe ☆ Not Fantasy ☆ A Mind-boggling Cosmology ☆ God's Method of Teaching Agape Love

"The Lame Take the Prey" ☆ Time — The Vestibule of Eternity ☆ The Broken Violin ☆ What Is Meant by Brokenness? ☆ Brokenness also Means Emptiness ☆ A Deeper Death to Self ☆ Explanation of the Mystery of Suffering ☆ Suffering — God's Grand Strategy ☆ Qualified Through Suffering ☆ Solomon's Temple ☆ Believers Are Living Stones ☆ The Shaping of the Stones

Earth, the Sphere of Learning Love ☆ Purity — Instantaneous ☆ Maturity — A Lifetime Process ☆ Life — A Laboratory ☆ Home — A Microcosm ☆ Newlyweds Often Self-centered ☆ A Spiritual Problem ☆ Learning Sacrificial Love ☆ Horizontal Versus Vertical ☆ The Right to Surrender Rights ☆ Repentance and Restitution ☆ An Insecure Foundation ☆ A Tragedy of Our Times ☆ A Professional Opinion ☆ An Atheistic Philosophy ☆ Seduction as Therapy ☆ Psychoanalysis Not a Science ☆ Integrity Therapy ☆ A Professional's Advice ☆ The Only Remedy ☆ Marital Unfaithfulness ☆ Overruling Moral Failures ☆ An Affirmation ☆ The Generation Gap

FOREWORD

Dear Brother Billheimer:

I was pleased indeed with the volume, *Destined for the Throne*, but I am thrilled with *Don't Waste Your Sorrows!* The insights and vantage points gained in the former volume have enabled you to see deeply and clearly into one of the darkest and most mysterious valleys of human existence — the problem of suffering and sorrow. You have no need of excusing it, for you show God using it as a precious means of developing character here and thereby making possible for the child of God as he enters the heavenly realm "a far more exceeding and eternal weight of glory."

Most materials written on the problem of sorrow leave the reader with questions. In this volume you give an answer clear, resounding, Biblical, and based on the character and being of God. The concept of God and man suffering together, and eternal values thereby accruing, impossible of achievement in any other way, helps to transmute sorrow and suffering into closer communion with the Lord.

Your idea of *agape* love transcends most treatments of the love motif by a unified treatment of its achievement here and its reward as rank in the Kingdom of God. *Don't Waste Your Sorrows* shows pain and suffering to be not an oversight or accident, but part of the eternal love-plan of God for perfecting "His family" on earth for their place in the eternal Kingdom of God.

In this century many millions of Christians have passed through suffering and death to receive a martyr's crown. There is no reason to doubt that millions of Christians now living may meet like persecution and martyrdom. *Don't Waste Your Sorrows* will prepare readers for unexpected testing and help them to rejoice when they suffer for Christ.

DR. B. H. PEARSON

Author, Missionary,
President Emeritus of World Gospel Crusades
Upland, California

INTRODUCTION

Today there is a strong emphasis in certain religious circles which insists that the ideal spiritual life is one of unbroken joy, peace, and material prosperity. The impression is current that to be saved and filled with the Spirit opens a charmed life entirely trouble-free, where all problems are instantaneously solved and where miracles never cease. According to some, "a miracle a day" is the norm. If one does not experience constant supernatural manifestations it is because he is subnormal spiritually. Something is wrong between him and God. To these people, the Spirit-filled life is one hilarious roller-coaster picnic and lark. No one should ever get sick, or, if he does, he should be healed immediately by simple effortless faith. If he needs money, all he has to do is ask God for it and the heavens open and down it pours. If anyone does not prosper and live affluently it is simply because he is not spiritually "on the ball." Some may feel that this is an exaggeration but it illustrates the point.

Facts indicate there is a significant measure of truth in this theology. Certainly it is true that few of us live up to our spiritual privilege. God would love to manifest His generosity and miracle-working power far more than is normally seen. But is this philosophy in proper spiritual perspective and balance or does it represent only one side of the coin?

The other side of the coin is represented by the concept

of the Christian life as a warfare that demands courage, sacrifice, and rugged self-discipline. This theology stresses the unavoidable weariness, toil, and pain that is sometimes encountered; the bitterness of conflict, the desperate days and grueling nights of darkness and distress. The following scriptures are illustrative: "Thou therefore endure hardness, as a good soldier of Jesus Christ" (2 Tim. 2:3). "If any man will come after me, let him deny himself, and take up his cross daily, and follow me" (Luke 9:23). "Then Jesus . . . said unto him, One thing thou lackest: go thy way, sell whatsoever thou hast, and give to the poor, and thou shalt have treasure in heaven: and come, take up the cross, and follow me" (Mark 10:21). "God forbid that I should glory, save in the cross of our Lord Jesus Christ" (Gal. 6:14).

This other side of the coin is also represented by the record of the noble army of martyrs whose blood has proved to be the seed of the Church. It is represented further by the body of literature that has exalted and glorified the heroic courage, valor, self-denial, and the high cost of discipleship or disciplined Christianity. What a contrast to some of the contemporary music is the following hymn:

> The Son of God goes forth to war,
> A kingly crown to gain;
> His blood red banner streams afar:
> Who follows in His train?
> Who best can drink His cup of woe,
> Triumphant over pain,
> Who patient bears the cross below,
> He follows in His train.
> — Reginald Heber

Amy Carmichael, who directed the Dohnavur Fellowship from an invalid's bed for many years, has articulated the warfare ideal in her Soldier's Prayer:

From prayer that asks that I may be
Sheltered from winds that beat on Thee,
From fearing when I should aspire,
From faltering when I should climb higher,
From silken self, O Captain, free
Thy soldier who would follow Thee.

From subtle love of softening things,
From easy choices, weakenings,
(Not thus are spirits fortified,
Not this way went the Crucified)
From all that dims Thy Calvary,
O Lamb of God, deliver me.

Give me the love that leads the way,
The faith that nothing can dismay,
The hope no disappointments tire,
The passion that will burn like fire,
Let me not sink to be a clod:
Make me Thy fuel, Flame of God. [1]

The soldier's theme has been immortalized by C. T. Studd in the following statement: "If Jesus Christ be God and died for me, then no sacrifice can be too great for me to make for Him."

Norman Grubb has pointed out that the Holy Spirit in the life of the believer will drive him to a life of suffering sacrifice just as He did in the life of Jesus.

In her book *What About Us Who Are Not Healed?* Mrs. Carmen Benson voices the doubts, fears, and perplexities of the multitudes who, without apparent reason, seek healing without success and mysteriously suffer on.

The question arises: Is the life of unbroken peace, joy, and prosperity, the life of health, happiness, and successful affluence, spiritually superior and the one which brings most glory to God? Are all who fall short of this ideal to be considered as second-class citizens of the kingdom? Must they be satisfied with the inferior rank of God's step-children?

One rejoices in the measure of faith that issues in success, in prosperity, and in healing. One recognizes that miracles of healing and other marvelous answers to prayer exalt our glorious Lord and His triumph over the adversary. The demonstration of the supernatural in signs and wonders is scriptural (2 Cor. 12:12) and confounds unbelief, stimulates faith in the hearts of God's people, and brings many souls to the Lord.

But HOW can the apparent failures be explained? A few are healed but the multitudes are not. A few have miraculous answers to prayer for healing and prosperity, but most do not. Are all those in this category to give up and wallow in self-pity and defeat? Is one to conclude that the multitudes who are not healed or delivered from grinding poverty must settle for second-class citizenship in the kingdom? Must the one who is not healed suffer with a sense of spiritual inferiority and the disappointing suspicion that he can have only God's second best while a select minority who are healed and blessed with affluence pass as ''God's chosen few''?

Or *is it possible for the great majority who remain financially limited or physically afflicted to make as great a contribution to the kingdom and bring as much joy to the heart of God and win as great an eternal reward as those who are favored with supernatural deliverance here and now?*

Is it conceivable that this question may be answered in the affirmative?

1. Amy Carmichael, *Gold Cord* (Fort Washington, PA: Christian Literature Crusade, 1974, and London: S.P.C.K., 1932), facing p. 1. Used by permission.

"For our light affliction, which is but for a moment, worketh for us a far more exceeding and eternal weight of glory; while we look not at the things which are seen, but at the things which are not seen: for the things which are seen are temporal; but the things which are not seen are eternal" (2 Corinthians 4:17-18).

"For our light, momentary affliction (this slight distress of the passing hour) is ever more and more abundantly preparing *and* producing *and* achieving for us an everlasting weight of glory — beyond all measure, excessively surpassing all comparisons and all calculations, a vast and transcendent glory and blessedness never to cease! Since we consider *and* look not to the things that are seen but to the things that are unseen; for the things that are visible are temporal (brief and fleeting), but the things that are invisible are deathless *and* everlasting" (2 Corinthians 4:17-18, *Amp.*).

That one's sorrows are actually working for the faithful believer is predicated upon the faith that the unseen is the ultimate and supreme reality and that the present and visible are only relative and ephemeral.

1

WHAT PRICE GLORY?

In order to understand this passage from 2 Corinthians 4 it is necessary to define the term "affliction." It is probable that Paul was thinking primarily about the persecutions, opposition, deprivations, and hardships which he and the early Christians faced in their devotion to and promotion of the gospel message.

Those which Paul himself suffered are partially detailed in 2 Corinthians 11:23-33. Among them were many experiences which produced physical suffering and possibly permanent injury. Many doubt that Paul's "thorn in the flesh" (2 Cor. 12:7) was physical illness, but that is not an impossible interpretation — in which case it too would be an affliction.

The original Greek word which is translated "affliction" simply means "pressure." According to *Webster's New World Dictonary*, "affliction" is "anything causing pain or distress." "It implies any sorrow, suffering, or heartache imposed by illness, loss, misfortune, etc."

Some believers conclude that God may use other types of affliction to discipline an erring saint or one who needs further child-training but not physical illness, because Jesus took upon Himself our infirmities and bore our pains upon the cross (Isa. 53:4-5).

Because of this they believe that it is *never* necessary for one to accept illness as disciplinary. Since the price has been paid for deliverance, they insist that a believer should be able to exercise faith for immediate healing without waiting to learn the new lesson God may be seeking to teach in the affliction.

This seems to be contrary to Paul's understanding in 1 Corinthians 11:28-32: "A man ought to examine himself before he eats of the bread and drinks of the cup. For anyone who eats and drinks without recognizing the body of the Lord eats and drinks judgment on himself. That is why many of you are weak and sick, and a number of you have fallen asleep. But if we judged ourselves, we would not come under judgment. When we are judged by the Lord, we are being disciplined so that we will not be condemned with the world" (*NIV*).

Here it seems that God is using physical affliction to discipline believers. If so, then it is impossible to rule out sickness as a means the Lord may use to focus the attention of a believer upon some area of his life which needs correction. Alexander Maclaren has said that every affliction comes with a message from the heart of God. Watchman Nee has said that we never learn anything new about God except by adversity. Again, David said, "Before I was afflicted [evidently physically] I went astray: but now have I kept thy word. It is good for me that I have been afflicted; that I might learn thy statutes" (Psalm 119:67,71). Finally, Job is an example of God's disciplinary use of physical affliction.

Thus it seems that although Jesus did take our infirmities and carry our pains, God does use physical affliction to chasten His children. If so, then we may not rule out sickness and disease as included in the "light affliction" which Paul says may work a far more exceeding and eternal weight of glory for the obedient and trusting child of God.

If we accept this interpretation of affliction, then Paul is saying that ''pressure'' from any cause, including bodily pain or suffering (even when no healing follows), may work for us. If this is possible, then believers who are suffering in the flesh and have failed to obtain healing should cease their lamentation, mourning, self-pity, and depression, and instead seek the method by which their suffering and sorrow may be transmuted into that ''eternal weight of glory.'' This book is an attempt to help the suffering find this method.

Life's Most Serious Problem

Except for sin, which is its cause, SORROW is life's most serious problem. According to *The New Testament and Wycliffe Bible Commentary* (page 665), the verb that is translated ''worketh,'' in the original also means ''create.'' This being true, the Apostle is saying that ''our light affliction,'' properly accepted, is actually creating or producing for us an ''eternal weight of glory'' far beyond all proportion to the pain of the affliction. Therefore it should be cherished and not *wasted* by resistance and rebellion.

Paul further amplifies this glorious truth of our thematic Scripture passage (2 Corinthians 4:17-18) in Romans 8:18, ''For I reckon that the sufferings of this present time are not worthy to be compared with the glory which shall be revealed in us.'' Also in Romans 5:3-5, ''We also rejoice in our sufferings, because we know that suffering produces perseverance; perseverance, character; and character, hope. And hope does not disappoint us, because God has poured out his love [agape love] into our hearts by the Holy Spirit, whom he has given to us'' (*NIV*).

To many people this is pure wishful thinking and its

acceptance is little more than "whistling in the dark." This book, based on solid logic and scriptural reality, is an attempt to show that this concept is more than just a morale builder.

Sorrow or suffering poses what has probably been in all ages the most serious problem for believers. Suffering is not only the last thing to be considered useful, but rather something to be avoided, evaded, and shunned. But, according to the Word of God, suffering is not an accident but a gift to be cherished, for when properly received it works to enhance one's eternal rank, fame, and honor.

Suffering Universal

In a fallen world, suffering of some kind is universal. There is no permanent release or escape from it, either by rank, holy living, health, or wealth. "Man is born unto trouble, as the sparks fly upward" (Job 5:7). "In the world ye shall have tribulation" (John 16:33). "But of course you know that such troubles are a part of God's plan for us Christians. Even while we were still with you we warned you ahead of time that suffering would soon come — and it did" (1 Thess. 3:3-4 *LB*). Trouble, therefore, comes to all, both saint and sinner.

The Sinner Has Sorrow

We are not surprised that the sinner has sorrow. "There will be trouble and distress for every human being who does evil" (Rom. 2:9 *NIV*). We understand that trouble and sorrow always follow sin. This is an immutable law. Although the sinner may fail to comprehend this, sin and sorrow are synonymous. "The wages of sin is death" (Rom. 6:23).

Why Does A Saint Suffer?

But *why* should the righteous suffer? Why isn't every believer healed, and healed immediately? Why isn't he "carried to the skies on flowery beds of ease"? Why must he "fight to win the prize and sail through bloody seas"? It is difficult for most people to understand why sorrow comes to a saint. That is one of the mysteries of the ages. However, regardless of the mystery involved, we know that God is love and that, according to 2 Corinthians 4:17-18, He permits suffering to the saint only to work (create) for him an "eternal weight of glory." No one ever becomes a saint without suffering because suffering, properly accepted, is the pathway to glory.

2

THE CHIEF SUFFERER IN THE UNIVERSE

The Suffering of the Godhead

Human beings are not the only sufferers in the universe. There is a tendency to suppose that the God who decreed the penalty for sin did so arbitrarily and is Himself unaffected by His decree. The supposition is that He is totally immune, entirely insulated from the suffering of the penalties He has imposed upon the sinning creation. The idea is widely accepted that He hurls His thunderbolts of wrath, that bring sorrow and heartbreak to others, from a so-called ivory tower of total isolation. Although He created a world in which sorrow now reigns, the accusation is made that He Himself sits scot-free, immune, untouched by its ravages and pangs.

But not so. You may be surprised by the statement that the infinitely happy God is the supreme sufferer in the universe. From all eternity, before He spoke the world into existence, before angels or archangels, cherubim or seraphim, before the first member of the human race was created in the image and likeness of God, God anticipated the Fall and ordained the plan of human redemption. And He knew this could not be accomplished without suffering to the Godhead. Nor could one worship as God one who is immune (sheltered) from suffering, because agape love, which is the essence of Godlike character, would then be lacking. It was the *slain Lamb,* the *One* who as man had suffered, who was acclaimed by the innumerable glorified throng of Revelation as worthy to receive power and riches and wisdom, strength, honor, glory, and blessing (Rev. 5:12).

God's Purpose — A Generic Family

God's original purpose in creation was to obtain a generic family of His very own, not created only, but also generated or begotten anew. "Long ago, even before he made the world, God chose us to be his very own [generically], through what Christ would do for us; he decided then to make us holy in his eyes, without a single fault — we who stand before him covered with his love. His unchanging plan has always been to adopt* us into his own family by sending Jesus Christ to die for us" (Eph. 1:4-5 *LB*). "For from the very beginning God decided that those who came to him — and all along he knew who would — should become like his Son, so that his Son would be the First, with many brothers" (Rom. 8:29 *LB*).

The Purpose of the Generic Family

But that was not all. The purpose of this generic family was to provide an Eternal Companion for the Son, called the Bride, the Lamb's Wife (Rev. 21:9). In God's plan this Eternal Companion is to be trained and elevated to the throne of the universe as co-regent with her Bridegroom following the Marriage Supper of the Lamb (Rev. 3:21, 19:7,9). But God knew that His Bride could not be obtained without infinite suffering to the Godhead. He also

---

*According to the *New Testament and Wycliffe Bible Commentary* (page 726) the term "adoption" in certain Bible passages is not used in the modern sense. Rather, it refers to one being placed in the position of a grown son. It is the formal and ceremonial recognition of a born son as having reached adulthood.

knew that the Bride could not be prepared for her queenly role without suffering to her. *If God was to realize His purpose in creation, to obtain an Eternal Companion for His Son, HE had to suffer.* It was unavoidable. *If the Bride was to be qualified to rule with Him, SHE also had to suffer.* This illuminates the passage in 2 Timothy 2:12, ''If we suffer, we shall also reign with him.'' *Therefore, suffering is inherent in God's universe.* Since this is true, suffering must be performing an infinitely valuable service. It must be of supreme importance.

Suffering Inherent in God's Economy

Because God wanted a voluntary love in His Bride-elect, He was compelled to give the Bridehood race an option. This option involved the possibility of the Fall. Sin requires redemption. Redemption requires the atonement. The atonement requires suffering. *Therefore, from all eternity, suffering is inherent in God's economy.*

The Cost of a Voluntary Love

When God conceived the plan of creation and redemption, He knew of the fall of mankind in advance and accepted the necessary fact of infinite suffering, of suffering Himself the total consequences of the cumulative sin of the world with its resultant sickness, sorrow, suffering, and pain. He knew He could not make a full atonement for sin without actually experiencing in His very own Being the full need of suffering which Eternal Justice would demand for the transgression of universal moral law. He therefore planned to come to earth as man, and it is of the God-man, Jesus, that we are informed: ''Who in the days of his flesh, when he had offered up prayers and supplications with strong crying and tears unto him that was able to save him from death, and was heard in that he feared; though he were a Son, yet learned he obedience by the things which he suffered'' (Heb. 5:7-8). *He also knew in advance that it*

(Heb. 2:10)

had to be in the same quality and intensity of suffering which accompanied the sin of the sinner.

Not a Bookkeeping Process

That the Godhead voluntarily accepted the certainty of suffering the full penalty and consequences of the cumulative sin of the race in order to obtain His Eternal Companion is therefore a logical and necessary corollary of the atonement. If Jesus did not actually experience in His own Person the full penalty of the sin of the race, the atonement would be merely a bookkeeping process which could in no way satisfy Eternal Justice. Eternal Justice could not survive if it merely ignored the sin of the race. Under universal jurisprudence the penalty of every sin of all mankind had to be paid by someone to balance the scales of the law's demands. This is why Christ, the Lamb of Revelation 13:8, is said to have been ''slain from the foundation of the world.'' Therefore, *suffering is inherent in a universe that is moral.*

3

A MORAL UNIVERSE

Three Kinds of Love

What is meant by a universe that is moral? *It is one in which the* Law of Love *is supreme, because love is the fulfilling of the law.* It fulfills every obligation to every intelligence in the universe, whether to God, man, or angelic beings. The most fundamental characteristic of an order that is moral, therefore, is *agape* love. There are three Greek words that are translated ''love'': *eros* — the love between the sexes; *philos* — the love of friendship; and *agape* — the love which characterizes God Himself. *Agape* love is the love which loves because of its own inherent nature, not because of the excellence or worth of its object. According to the Bible dictionary it is spontaneous, automatic love. To illustrate: the sun shines alike upon fragrant flower gardens and reeking dung heaps because it is its nature to shine. It cannot help it. Just so, God's love embraces good and evil personalities alike, pouring out His blessings of sunshine and rain equally upon the just and the unjust (Matt. 5:45). *''God is love''* (1 John 4:8). He is personified love. He consists of love which is His essence. 1 Corinthians 13 is a divinely inspired description of *agape* love. *Agape* love is not primarily an emotion but aggressive, benevolent, sacrificial outgoing goodwill. It is the soul of ethics.

The Omnipotence of Love

Because God is (agape) love, *then love must be the one all-powerful principle in the universe. Otherwise God could not be God.* The syllogism would be stated thus: God is all powerful. God is love. Therefore love is all powerful. *Since this is true, then love is the all-enduring, everlasting, supreme principle of the universe.* Satan challenged this principle and lost. According to Revelation 12, there was war in heaven and Satan and his angels were cast out. However, he still believes that brute force is more powerful than love. He is the power behind the beast of Revelation and, according to modern Satanism, still expects to dethrone God.

According to *The Satanic Bible,* the crucifix symbolizes ''pallid incompetence hanging on a tree.'' In *The Satanic Rituals,* Satan is called ''the ineffable Prince of Darkness who rules the earth.'' He is further seen as seizing the initiative from Christ, who is called ''the lasting foulness of Bethlehem,'' ''the cursed Nazarene,'' ''impotent king,'' ''fugitive and mute God,'' ''vile and abhorred pretender to the majesty of Satan.''

Satan is described as ''Lucifer who rules the earth'' and who will send the ''Christian minions staggering to their doom.'' He is also depicted as the ''Lord of Light'' — with Christ's angels, cherubim, and seraphim, ''cowering and trembling with fear'' and ''prostrating themselves before him,'' while he ''sends the gates of heaven crashing down.''

The Ultimate Triumph of Love

The Book of Revelation tells a different story. It describes a conflict between a wild beast, representing brute force, and a slain Lamb. The conflict ends with the beast forever banished and the Lamb on the throne of the universe with the Bride at His side as co-regent. *Love has won!* When the heavens shall pass away with a great noise, and the elements shall melt with fervent heat, and the earth and the works that are in it shall be burned up; when "hoary time shall pass away and earthly thrones and kingdoms fall"; when the new heavens and the new earth in which dwells righteousness replace a ruined and purged universe, only that which has come to terms with love will remain. *This love is even now, this present throbbing moment, the supreme law of the universe and will survive and outlast all its rivals.*

The Purpose of Life on Earth

Because this is true, learning agape love as personified in Christ is the supreme purpose of life on earth. This is the meaning of all that God permits to come to one of His children. *God's primary occupation in this age is not regulating the universe by "the mighty power of His command," but it is teaching the members of His Bride-elect the lessons of agape love in preparation for the throne.* He is doing nothing in the realm of redemption that is not related to this task. Therefore, every single incident, whether of joy or sorrow, bane or blessing, pain or pleasure, without exception is being utilized by God for the purpose of procuring the members of His Bridehood and maturing them in agape love. *Thus, the supreme purpose of life on earth is not pleasure, fame, wealth, or any other form of worldly success, but learning agape love. In the ultimate social order of the universe (the kingdom of God) rank will be determined, not by talent, magnetic personality, intellectual acumen, earthly success and affluence, but by one thing and one alone — agape love.*

"Jesus said, Ye know that the princes of the Gentiles exercise dominion over them, and they that are great exercise authority upon them. But it shall not be so among you: but whosoever will be great among you, let him be your minister; and whosoever will be chief among you, let him be your servant; even as the Son of man came not to be ministered unto, but to minister, and to give his life a ransom for many'' (Matt. 20:25-28).

Love Suffers

There is no love without self-giving. There is no self-giving without pain. Therefore, there is no love without suffering. *Suffering is an essential ingredient of agape love and therefore of a moral universe.* Even God cannot love without cost. If you think that the infinitely happy God cannot suffer, think what it must have cost Him to give His Son to die as a sinner and a sin offering on the cross. Think what it must have cost Him to turn His face away from His innocent Son and forsake Him who did no sin but who, for our sakes, *became sin* (2 Cor. 5:21). Think also what it must have cost Him to see the Son of His love descend into hell and be delivered to the torments of Satan and the demons for their pleasure (Eph. 4:9 and Acts 2:27). And think what it must have cost Him to pour out upon Him — on the cross and in hell — the full fury of His own wrath against sin because of the guilt of the cumulative sin of all mankind (Heb. 2:9). [1]

Love Suffers Voluntarily

The Apostle Paul said, ''Love suffers'' (1 Cor. 13:4). This means that love must suffer voluntarily. God is love, but there is no love without voluntary suffering. Love that does not accept suffering voluntarily is a misnomer, for the essence of love is decentralization, that is, repudiation of self in behalf of another. There is no decentralization without voluntary acceptance of suffering. *Therefore, in the universal absolute sense, there is no character without suffering. Suffering love is the cornerstone of the universe because without it there is no decentralization of the self and therefore no agape love.* One who has never voluntarily suffered is totally selfish. *Only great sufferers are truly benevolent. There is no such thing as a saint who has not suffered.*

NOTES

1. See Paul E. Billheimer, *Destined for the Throne* (Fort Washington, PA: Christian Literature Crusade, 1975), chapter 6.

4

LEGAL DELIVERANCE

Legal Deliverance Through Christ's Sufferings

Because Christ could not make a full atonement for sin without absorbing its full consequences in His own Person and Being, no human being can ever suffer a pain, sorrow, heartache, or disappointment that Christ has not already experienced in His own Person.

Isaiah 53, the great atonement chapter, affirms: "Surely he hath borne *our* griefs, and carried *our* sorrows: . . . he was wounded for our transgressions, he was bruised for our iniquities: the chastisement of our peace was upon him; and with his stripes we are healed" (Isa. 53:4-5). In the context of Christ's healing ministry, Matthew translates this: "Himself took *our* infirmities, and bore *our* sicknesses" (Matt. 8:17).

Verse 6 of Isaiah 53 states: "All we like sheep have gone astray; we have turned every one to his own way; and the Lord hath laid upon *him* the iniquity of us all." Therefore, the total penalty, all the sorrow, suffering, pain, poverty, and disease, the full consequences of the cumulative sins of all of Adam's race, was laid upon Him. What is the meaning of all this for the suffering believer? *It means that every born-again believer is legally delivered from the full penalty, all the bitter fruits of sin and the fall. This penalty cannot legally be collected the second time.* The prophet said, "By his stripes we are healed." *If so, then every believer is legally delivered from all sickness, disease, pain, sorrow, poverty, and limitations of every kind.*

What Is Legal Deliverance?

CRITICAL AXIOM

Through Adam's fall all of his progeny became bona fide slaves of Satan. He possessed the power of death over them. But because Jesus was born of the Virgin Mary without human father, and so was not a mere son of Adam, Satan had no legal right to touch Him. Previously, Satan had slain his millions with impunity. When he *illegally* slew Jesus upon the cross, for the first time in history Satan legally became a murderer. This brought upon him the sentence of death. A person under the sentence of death has no legal standing, rights, or claims. He is legally destroyed. This is what the writer to the Hebrews meant when he said that through death Jesus destroyed (rendered powerless) "him that had the power of death, that is, the devil" (Heb. 2:14). Therefore, since Calvary, Satan has *no legal authority* over any believer. The believer's faith has translated him out of the kingdom of darkness (Satan's authority), into the kingdom of God's dear Son (Col. 1:13).

Although Satan is legally destroyed, and has no lawful authority over the believer, God uses him as an opponent to train the Bride-elect in overcoming and *in learning agape love.* Thus, when God allows Satan to afflict one of His children, it is not because Satan has any legal right to do so, but in order to train God's child in overcoming and in learning deeper dimensions of agape love. Because Satan lost all of his claims at Calvary, every child of God is legitimately delivered from all of his affliction and oppresssion. *All that God permits to remain is only for child-training purposes.* The Apostle Paul understood this when he said that our light affliction is working for us (2 Cor. 4:17-18).

When one is delivered from affliction by faith here and now, he has triumphed. When the symptoms persist and he has learned a new dimension of agape love, he has also triumphed because he has increased his eternal rank.

The Universal Scope of the Atonement

In the Word, therefore, there is a perfect theology of health and prosperity. From Genesis to Revelation run the glad tidings that the atonement covers the entire scope of human need. The more than 32,000 promises assure us that all we need for body, soul, and spirit for both time and eternity is provided in the atonement. Nothing could be more sweeping than Philippians 4:19, ''My God shall supply all your need according to his riches in glory by Christ Jesus.'' Also 3 John 2, ''Beloved, I wish above all things that thou mayest prosper and be in health, even as thy soul prospereth.'' These promises are amplified and supported by thousands of others guaranteeing health and prosperity to God's obedient people.

A Clear Theology of Health and Prosperity

From the beginning God promised both temporal and spiritual blessings to Israel as long as she was obedient. ''If thou wilt diligently hearken to the voice of the Lord thy God, and wilt do that which is right in his sight, and wilt give ear to his commandments, and keep all his statutes, I will put none of these diseases upon thee, which I have brought upon the Egyptians; for I am the Lord that healeth thee'' (Ex. 15:26). Also read Leviticus 26:3-10 and Deuteronomy chapter 28.

The theme is continued in the record of the healing miracles of Jesus in the Gospels, in those of the Apostles in Acts, and reaches a distinct confirmation in James 5:14-15: ''Is any sick among you? let him call for the elders of the church; and let them pray over him, anointing him with oil in the name of the Lord; and the prayer of faith shall save the sick, and the Lord shall raise him up; and if he have committed sins, they shall be forgiven him.''

The Early Church — God's Prototype

It appears there is as distinct a theology in the Word for health and prosperity as there is for salvation. Many believe that the first century Church is God's prototype for the entire age, that we are still in the dispensation of the Holy Spirit, and that if God had His way, all the gifts of the Spirit would be present and manifest in the Church today in a similar proportion as in the early Church. Many are convinced from the Word that health and prosperity are God's first and best choice for His obedient children. All other things being equal, He would prefer our health to our illness.

How could it be otherwise? The Lord taught His disciples to pray: ''Thy will be done in earth, as it is in heaven'' (Matt. 6:10). We are sure there is no sickness or poverty in that fair land. Since these are the result of sin, they cannot be God's preferential will because sin and all of its effects are against the will of God. HALLELUJAH! The entire universe is moving toward a social order called the kingdom of God, where none of these can exist (Rev. 21:4-5 and 22:2-5). Therefore, they cannot be God's choice at any time for any part of His dominion. *All of God's universe-wide activity is directed toward the total elimination of sin and all of its consequences from all spheres of His redeemed creation.*

Since all of these things are true, *why* should any obedient child of God suffer? Not because God wills it as such, nor because He has not made provision for its eradication, *but because the ultimate goal of the universe is a social order where agape love is supreme.*

When God wants to drill a man
  And thrill a man
  And skill a man,
When God wants to mold a man
  To play the noblest part;
When He yearns with all His heart
  To create so great and bold a man
That all the world shall be amazed,
  Watch His methods, watch His ways!
How He ruthlessly perfects
  Whom He royally elects!
How He hammers him and hurts him,
  And with mighty blows converts him
Into trial shapes of clay which
  Only God understands;
While his tortured heart is crying
  And he lifts beseeching hands!
How He bends but never breaks
  When his good He undertakes;
How He uses whom He chooses
  And with every purpose fuses him;
  By every act induces him
To try His splendor out—
  God knows what He's about!

5

THE MYSTERY OF SUFFERING

Love the Norm of the Universe

God is calling and preparing an Eternal Companion called the Bride, who is to sit with His Son on His throne as His co-regent in the ages to come (Rev. 3:21). In order to qualify for this exalted position the members of the Bridehood *must* be as nearly like the Son as it is possible for the finite to be like the infinite. If they are to qualify for their lofty duties they *must* share the character of God Himself which is agape love. *This is the norm of the universe,* the ideal toward which God is working for the eternal social order. But as we have seen, that quality of character cannot be developed in fallen humanity without suffering (see Chapter 3).

Glory and Suffering

This explains Paul's inspired revelation: "If we suffer, we shall also reign with him" (2 Tim. 2:12). According to Romans 5:3-5 suffering issues in character (agape love), and character is a prerequisite to rulership. Because there is no character development without suffering, suffering is a necessary preparation for rulership.

Massive Damage of the Fall

God pronounced unfallen Adam "very good," but the Fall brought massive damage to Adam and all of his progeny. It left the race self-centered. Self-centeredness is the very essence of all sin and misery and results in self-destruction. It is the core of hostility, and hostility is the core of hell, the *hallmark* and essence of hell. Self-centeredness is the antithesis of holiness or agape love, the hallmark and essence of heaven.

The Necessity of Decentralization

In bringing an individual into the likeness of His Son, God must decentralize him. Decentralization begins in the crisis of justification and the new birth and continues in the crisis of sanctification or the filling with the Holy Spirit. Of necessity it does not end there. These are only beginning experiences similar to a vestibule which is a good place to enter but a poor place to stay. The work of sanctification by which the self is decentralized is both instantaneous and progressive. It is both a crisis and a process which continues throughout life. ''And I am sure that God who began the good work within you will keep right on helping you grow in his grace until his task within you is finally finished on that day when Jesus Christ returns'' (Phil. 1:6 *LB*).

The Work of Tribulation

If God's net purpose in saving an individual is just to get him to heaven, He would probably take him to glory immediately. But God wants to prepare him for rulership in an infinite universe that demands character. Progress in sanctification, in the development of Godlike character and agape love, is impossible without tribulation and chastisement. ''Not only so, but we also rejoice in our sufferings, because we know that suffering produces perseverance; perseverance, character; and character, hope. And hope does not disappoint us, because God has poured out his love into our hearts by the Holy Spirit, whom he has given us'' (Rom. 5:3-5 *NIV*). ''My son, don't be angry when the Lord punishes you. Don't be discouraged when he has to show you where you are wrong. For when he punishes you, it proves that he loves you. When he whips you it proves that you are really his child. Let God train you, for he is doing what any loving father does for his children. Whoever heard of a son who was never corrected? If God doesn't punish you when you need it, as other fathers punish their sons, then it means that you aren't really God's son at all — that you don't really belong in his family. . . . Our earthly fathers trained us for a few brief years, doing the best for us that they knew how, but God's correction is always right and for our best good, that we may share his holiness [character]. Being punished isn't enjoyable while it is happening — it hurts! But afterwards we can see the result, *a quiet growth in grace and character*" (Heb. 12:5b-8, 10-11 *LB* — Italics mine).

> I walked a mile with pleasure;
> She chattered all the way,
> But left me none the wiser
> For all she had to say.
>
> I walked a mile with sorrow;
> And ne'er a word said she;
> But, O, the things I learned from her
> When sorrow walked with me.

Chastisement and Child Training

It is clear from the foregoing and other similar passages of Scripture that sorrow, suffering, tribulation, and pain which come to the believer are not primarily for punishment but for child training. They are not purposeless. Earthly parents may make mistakes in their chastisement — and often do. But not God. He is preparing the believer for rulership in a universe so vast that it appears infinite. It seems that God cannot fully decentralize fallen man, even though born again, sanctified or filled with the Holy Spirit, without suffering. Watchman Nee says that we never learn anything new about God except through adversity. Some consider this an exaggeration, but it does seem that few seek a deeper walk with God except under duress.

Example of Israel

The history of Israel illustrates this point. In prosperity she forsook pure Jehovah worship for licentious idolatry. Only by chastisement was she constrained to repent and return to Jehovah. For centuries, while God was seeking to obtain a pure remnant through whom He could bring the Messiah, it was the same routine: prosperity, backsliding, and apostasy; chastisement, repentance, and return to God ad infinitum (Judg. 2:11-19; 1 Sam. 12:9-10; 2 Chron. 15:4, 33:12; Isa. 26:16).

Example of the Psalmist

The experience of the Psalmist is illustrative: "Before I was afflicted I went astray: but now I have kept thy Word. It is good for me that I have been afflicted; that I might learn thy statutes" (Psalm 119:67, 71). Who of us have not known people with Christian background and training who have wandered far from God and have been brought back to Him through heart attack, cancer, tragic accident, or some other severe affliction?

Example of Christ

One of the most amazing commentaries on the purposefulness of suffering in the economy of God is set forth in Hebrews 2:10: "For it became him, for whom are all things, and by whom are all things, in bringing many sons unto glory, to make the captain of their salvation *perfect through sufferings*." "Though he were a Son, yet learned he obedience *by the things which he suffered*" (Heb. 5:8). In Christ's case, according to Maclaren, "His perfecting was not the perfecting of moral character but the completion of His equipment for His work as Leader and Originator of our salvation. Before He suffers He has the pity of God. After He suffers He has the compassion of a man."[1] *The New Testament and Wycliffe Bible Commentary* says: "By suffering his *human* experience was made complete. . . . Because he suffered he is now fully qualified to serve as captain (*archegos,* leader) of man's salvation."[2] If the "many sons" whom Christ was to bring to glory and rulership had to be prepared and perfected for that glory by suffering, their Captain must lead the way by having His human experience perfected in the same way. The fact that Christ's human experience had to be perfected by suffering proves that no suffering is purposeless, but that it is endemic in God's economy.

The Importance of Brokenness

Christ's suffering only matured and perfected His human experience. It purged nothing from His moral nature even as a man because He was unfallen. No stain of sin ever marred His humanity. But not so with fallen man. There is no way that Christlike character can be formed in man without suffering because he cannot be decentralized otherwise. If he will not suffer, if he determines to evade it, if he refuses to allow the life of nature and of self to go to the cross, to that extent he will remain hard, self-centered, unbroken, and therefore unChristlike. "Whole, unbruised, unbroken men are of little use to God" (J. R. Miller). By his self-will one may escape a certain quality of pain, that which accompanies voluntary self-immolation, but in so doing he becomes the victim of a far greater pain, that of self-worship. He cannot escape both. Someone has said, "There are things which even God cannot do for us unless He allows us to suffer.''

The Pain of Moral Choice

Oswald Chambers says that ''God does not make us holy in the sense of character; He makes us holy in the sense of innocence, and we have to turn that innocence into holy character by a series of moral choices. These choices are continually in antagonism to the entrenchments of our natural life.'' [3]

There can be no spiritual progress, therefore, except through the progressive death of the self-life. Maclaren has said that every step on the pathway of spiritual progress will be marked by the bloody footprints of wounded self-love. All along the course of spiritual advancement one will have to set up altars upon which even the legitimate self-life will have to be sacrificed.

To make the moral choices that develop Godlike character always causes pain because even after one has been sanctified, filled with the Holy Spirit, one is still fallen. Some people feel that after these experiences of grace, nothing remains in their spiritual life with which God has a controversy. But the work of sanctification is both instantaneous and progressive. It will continue until glorification.

Sheridan Baker, a writer in the early holiness movement, has said: ''But there is much to be done for the believer in the way of chastening, and melting, and mellowing, after this state [the Spirit's baptism] is reached, and consequently, it is not a finality in the process of redemption. . . . The purified believer will not be long in discovering rudeness in his manners which he will deplore and escape, roughness in his speech and tone of voice which he will deprecate and abandon, and other dregs of the old disease which will cling to him, though the disease itself has been removed and from which he will escape 'by little and little' as beautifully symbolized by the conquest of Canaan.''[4]

The Spiritually Static State a Vice

One of the greatest vices of the Church is a static state of grace. The fruit of a grapevine is always on the new growth. This is the reason for pruning the vine. Without new growth there is little or no fruit. This is why Jesus said, ''Every branch that beareth fruit, he purgeth [prunes] it, that it may bring forth more fruit'' (John 15:2). If the branch had sensibility, pruning would be painful. But without suffering there would be neither growth nor fruitfulness.

Annie Johnson Flint has beautifully expressed this truth:

> It is the branch that bears the fruit,
>   That feels the knife
> To prune it for a larger growth,
>   A fuller life.
>
> Though every budding twig be lopped,
>   And every grace
> Of swaying tendril, springing leaf,
>   Be lost a space,
>
> O thou whose life of joy seems reft,
>   Of beauty shorn;
> Whose aspirations lie in dust,
>   All bruised and torn,
>
> Rejoice, tho' each desire, each dream,
>   Each hope of thine
> Shall fall and fade; it is the hand
>   Of Love Divine
>
> That holds the knife, that cuts and breaks
>   With tenderest touch,
> That thou, whose life has borne some fruit
>   May'st now bear much.

Self-pity a Waste

How meaningful are the words of Jesus in John 15:1, ''My Father is the husbandman'' — not Satan, but *My Father*. Not understanding God's benevolent purpose, when sorrow and suffering come — whether as the result of conflict over moral choices, of pain and physical illness, or of disappointing circumstances — it is easy to fall into a spirit of resentment and self-pity which produces frustration and depression. When this occurs one is defeated in his spiritual life, and character deteriorates. *He has wasted his sorrow.* What God permitted in order to wean him from self-love and self-worship, and therefore for his spiritual growth, has resulted in loss.

Comfort from Pain

How often one is tempted to question, even mourn the years of disability, invalidism, and pain suffered by saints such as Madame Guyon, Fanny Crosby, Amy Carmichael, George Matheson, and others, out of whose suffering God distilled sweet comfort, healing, and strength for millions of fainting pilgrims. God's frequent transmutation of sorrow into blessing for others is beautifully expressed in these lines:

> Out of the presses of pain
> Cometh the soul's best wine;
> And the eyes that have shed no rain
> Can shed but little shine.

This, of course, illustrates only the temporal situation, not the eternal weight of glory which is perceived only as one fastens his vision upon ''things that are not seen.''

Character from Affliction

Suffering, from whatever source, of whatever nature, and of whatever intensity, plus triumphant acceptance equals character (Rom. 5:3-4). Character (agape love) is the coin, the legal tender of heaven. Therefore, "our light affliction which is but for a moment, is working for us a far more exceeding and eternal weight of glory," that is, an exceedingly higher rank. Affliction, triumphantly accepted here, means rank there because this is the way God builds selfless character and develops agape love. Suffering, triumphantly accepted, slays the self-life, delivers one from self-centeredness, and frees one to love.

Those who have thus suffered will form the elite, the aristocracy, the ruling nobility of the future. They will constitute the princes of the ethereal realm.

Blessed Be Sorrow

In order to grow in character it is necessary to understand that nothing that God permits to come to His child, whether "good" or "ill," is accidental or without design. Everything is intended to drive him out of himself into God. "All life is intended to be a pathway to God" (Maclaren). All is for the purpose of character training. *There are no exceptions.* God never slumbers nor sleeps (Psalm 121:4). Because God is the all-seeing One, Satan cannot "slip up on His blind side." He is never taken by surprise. Only this faith will enable one to understand the statement: "Blessed be sorrow."

Blessed Be Frustration and Pain

God cannot train one without mystifying him, without baffling him. Evidently God has objectives in us which cannot be achieved apart from frustration and bewildering pain. *Faith cannot be perfected except by apparent denial.* This was the way Job's faith was perfected so that he said, "Though he slay me, yet will I trust in him" (Job 13:15). This is the kind of faith that does not depend upon tangible fulfillment. It cannot be developed without being utterly baffled. God cannot develop this quality of faith in one without apparently denying Himself. Indeed, He may sometimes need to appear to be false as in the case of Job. Or, He may sometimes need to seem faithless as in the case of Abraham offering up Isaac when God's promise and command appeared to be in diametric opposition. In Abraham's case faith was led to the very edge of the precipice. And this meant suffering, probably the most unendurable of all. Until one has weathered this kind of testing and trial of faith, he cannot identify with the author of the following lines:

> I will not doubt, though all my ships at sea
>   Come drifting home with broken masts and sails;
>   I will believe the hand which never fails,
> From seeming evil worketh good for me.
>   And though I weep because those sails are tattered,
>   Still will I cry, while my best hopes lie shattered:
>   "I trust in Thee."
>
> I will not doubt, though sorrows fall like rain,
>   And troubles swarm like bees about a hive.
>   I will believe the heights for which I strive
> Are only reached by anguish and by pain;
>   And though I groan and writhe beneath my crosses,
>   I yet shall see through my severest losses
>   The greater gain.

The Mystery of Healing Failures

This is the kind of suffering which plagues many who are seeking healing. They realize there is a perfect theology of healing. They know that the atonement is full and complete. They fully believe that Jesus Himself has borne their sicknesses and carried their pains. They are convinced that they are legally delivered from every oppression of the devil. Yet the faith that brings actual deliverance from the symptoms seems unobtainable. Sometimes this goes on for years and even unto death. Some are healed but many are not. Some are given achieving faith and are miraculously restored. Many, however, are not.

NOTES

1. Alexander Maclaren, *Exposition of Hebrews*, p. 234.

2. *The New Testament and Wycliffe Bible Commentary* (Chicago: Moody Press. Copyright © 1971, The Iversen-Norman Associates, New York), p. 909.

3. Oswald Chambers, *My Utmost for His Highest* (New York: Dodd, Mead & Company, 1935), p. 252. Used by permission.

4. Sheridan Baker, *Hidden Manna* (Chicago and Boston: The Christian Witness Co., 1903), pp. 51,53.

6

A FAITH GREATER THAN ACHIEVING FAITH

The Greatest Eternal Profit

Until recently, during all of my lengthy ministry, I have been under the solid impression that supernatural healing and deliverance here and now *always* brings more glory to God and more eternal profit to the individual than continued suffering. For those who are healed this is probably true. A sovereign God knows what He is doing. But for those who are not healed, may it not be otherwise? There is something to be said for this viewpoint. If the goal of the universe is character — that is, a disposition of agape love — and if character cannot be created without tribulation, then may not the discipline of tribulation produce in both time and eternity as desirable a result, if not a better one? *The answer lies in our reaction to the discipline.* Resentment and rebellion only *waste one's sorrows,* whereas humble acceptance and brokenness allows the creation of an ''eternal weight of glory.''

Great Sainthood Often Means Great Suffering

It is not unusual that the greatest saints, those who have made the greatest contribution to the kingdom on earth, are those who have suffered the most. The world never would have heard of Madame Guyon and the Church never would have been enriched by the fragrance of her life, and perhaps eternity would have been poorer if it had not been for her victory over tribulation. If ever a person could have *wasted her sorrow,* it was she. By the depth of her triumphant submission, her sufferings were transmuted into character which has left an indelible mark upon the spiritual life of succeeding generations and probably, more significantly, enriched heaven. Among those influenced by her life and witness was the sainted Fenelon. Would it have been better for the kingdom, would it have brought more glory to Christ, would her eternal rank have been more exalted, if Madame Guyon had been healed of smallpox and spared the crushing humiliation and sorrows that followed in its wake?

A Deep Dimension of Agape Love Greater Than Mountain-moving Faith

It seems possible, even probable, that Madame Guyon's eternal worth and service, her contribution to the eternal kingdom, was enhanced more by the way she was enabled to triumph in adversity of every kind, especially ill health, than it would have been if she had been miraculously healed. It seems possible that the completeness of her submission and triumphant faith in the wisdom and goodness of her adorable Lord brought more joy and satisfaction to His heart than would have a miracle-working faith for healing and deliverance. *The faith that can truly say "Though He slay me yet will I trust Him" may be more precious in God's sight than faith that moves mountains because it may arise out of a more self-sacrificial love.* The words of the great Apostle support this: "Though I speak with the tongues of men and of angels, and have not *love,* I am become as sounding brass, or a tinkling cymbal. And though I have the gift of prophecy, and understand all mysteries, and all knowledge; *and though I have all faith, so that I could remove mountains,* *and have not love, I am nothing''* (1 Cor. 13:1-2). It was Madame Guyon's unutterable love for her Lord that enabled her to triumph over suffering, pain, and unspeakable misfortune, including the loss by death of her children and loved ones.*

Could it be that the many others who seek and fail to find healing have as great or greater opportunity to glorify God by accepting suffering triumphantly, as she did, and developing the character of agape love which is the legal tender of heaven?

Heroes of Faith of Hebrews Eleven

Hebrews eleven may illuminate this question. From verse 32 through the first part of verse 35 is the record of the heroes of faith who were gloriously, miraculously, and supernaturally delivered. There is nothing like it outside the annals of sacred history. Among other spectacular deliverances recorded, such as those of Daniel from the

---

* "To resume my history, the smallpox had so much hurt one of my eyes, that it was feared I would lose it. The gland at the corner of my eye was injured. An imposthume arose from time to time between the nose and the eye, which gave me great pain till it was lanced. It swelled all my head to that degree that I could not bear even a pillow. The least noise was agony to me, though sometimes they made a great commotion in my chamber. Yet this was a precious time to me, for two reasons. First, because I was left in bed alone, where I had a sweet retreat without interruption; the other, because it answered the desire I had for suffering — which desire was so great, that all the austerities of the body would have been but as a drop of water to quench so great a fire. Indeed the severities and rigors which I then exercised were extreme, but they did not appease this appetite for the cross. It is Thou alone, O Crucified Saviour, who canst make the cross truly effectual for the death of self. Let others bless themselves in their ease or gaity, grandeur or pleasures, poor temporary heavens; for me, my desires were all turned another way, even to the silent path of suffering for Christ, and to be united to Him, through the mortification of all that was of nature in me, that my senses, appetites and will, being dead to these, might wholly live in Him." [1]

lion's den and the Three Hebrew Children from the fiery furnace, mention is made of supernatural healing when "weakness was turned to strength" (vs. 34 *NIV*), and others were raised from the dead (vs. 35a).

But another order of heroes of faith is listed beginning in the middle of verse 35: "Others were tortured, not accepting deliverance; that they might obtain a better resurrection: and others had trial of cruel mockings and scourgings, yea, moreover of bonds and imprisonment: they were stoned, they were sawn asunder, were tempted, were slain with the sword: they wandered about in sheepskins and goatskins; being destitute, afflicted, tormented" (vss. 35b-37). According to verse 39, these also "were all commended for their faith, yet none of them received what had been promised" (*NIV*).

The Heroism of Faithful Endurance

Does anyone believe that those who were delivered were more highly commended for their faith than those who were not? Does anyone doubt that as high or higher a degree of love was demonstrated by those who suffered but endured without deliverance, as by those who enjoyed the miraculous? Because the law of love is supreme in the eternal social order, is it not possible that the army of saints who proved their sacrificial love by "climbing the steep ascent to heaven through peril, toil, and pain," wandering about "in sheepskins and goatskins, living in dens and caves of the earth" — is it not possible that they may be of equal rank with those who were miraculously delivered? Because agape love is the legal tender of heaven, when the rewards are meted out in that day, may it not be that those who joyfully "drank their cup of woe" by enduring destitution, affliction, and torment may be of comparable or higher rank than those who escaped by supernatural intervention?

What Is Suffering *With* Christ?

We usually think of the afflictions which Paul says are "working for us an eternal weight of glory" as probably in the category of severe persecution or martyrdom. It has been said that in the last twenty-five years more people have suffered severe persecution and martyrdom for Christ than in any other similar period of history. Some of us may yet be called upon to prove our faith and love by accepting a martyr's crown. But at this point, in the United States, the adversity to which most believers are subject is not the danger of martyrdom or other types of persecution practiced in Communist lands. Today the American believer's afflictions are mostly physical, financial, or in the area of personality conflicts. Is this type suffering included in "these light afflictions" which Paul said are working for us? Is this what he meant when he said "if we suffer we shall also reign" and "if so be that we suffer, that we may be glorified together"?

The answer may be that it is not always the character of the affliction which determines its spiritual value but rather the length of its continuation and one's reaction to it. Whether the suffering is for and *with* Christ may be determined not so much by its nature and severity as by the quality of one's spirit in which it is faced. For example, to live sweetly with a brute of a man, or a contentious, faithless woman, or an ungrateful, contemptuous, wayward son or daughter, or to live self-sacrificially with a helpless, hopeless invalid for years or for a lifetime, may provide the opportunity to develop martyr strength and a deep dimension of love as truly as severe persecution for Christ's sake.

All affliction is intended to drive one to God. It is intended to work a fuller submission, a more utter devotion, an increasing patience, a greater beauty of spirit, a more selfless love toward both God and man. When it accomplishes this, then it may be classified as suffering *with* Christ and for His sake because it has enabled Him to achieve His end and purpose in that one. It may require a lifetime of God's dealing in discipline and chastisement to produce the true martyr spirit. When suffering of any character is allowed to work in one a deeper dimension of agape love, is it not indeed "suffering with Christ"?

The Triumph of Submission

May affliction which one is now suffering, and from which he has long and earnestly sought relief, enable him to join the noble army of the heroes of faith in Hebrews eleven? Is it possible that one may join that noble band by facing his illness or other self-crucifying situations in submission and triumph? It seems that Madame Guyon did just that. If the spirit in which she faced and triumphed over her afflictions and sorrows brought more glory to Christ than her deliverance would have, is it not possible that others who are not delivered may do likewise by the way they face their difficulties? May not the multitudes who seek and fail to receive healing, by a proper subjective attitude of submission and courage in their afflictions, transmute them into "a far more exceeding and eternal weight of glory" as did those in Hebrews eleven? The answer is "yes" when they demonstrate a like victory over tribulation.

The Heroism of Patient Plodding

It seems to some that a life which is ended swiftly by an act of martyrdom may be more heroic and a greater testimony of deathless love than a long life of faithfulness in the ordinary trials and tribulations of daily life. But may it not be that God is obtaining a similar quality of selfless devotion and sacrificial love through patient endurance of the routine sorrow, suffering, disappointments, heartaches, and pain which He permits as a part of His loving child-training? If so, then those who suffer triumphantly, accepting the "things that hurt and things that mar" with submission, thanksgiving, and praise, may be enhancing their eternal rank in a similar way as did the martyrs. *By a proper reaction while in the school of suffering, they may be learning and demonstrating a quality of agape love which is preparing them for rulership as truly as though they had suffered martyrdom.*

On the other hand, *yeilding to self-pity, depression, and rebellion is a waste of sorrow.* Those who have unsuccessfully sought healing and who submit to resentment, discontent, impatience, and bitterness against God *are wasting what God intended for growth in love and thus for enhanced rank in the eternal kingdom.*

NOTES

1. Madame Guyon, *Madame Guyon* (*Autobiography*) (Chicago: Moody Press), pp. 140-141.

7

THE GREAT BUSINESS OF LIFE —
LEARNING AGAPE LOVE

Nominees for Exalted Rank

Maybe God cannot get some of the rare saints He needs for certain exclusive and highly specialized vocations in His eternal kingdom any other way than by permitting them to suffer catastrophic losses, sorrow, and pain. If so, then those who have sought healing in vain while others around them are delivered, need not abandon themselves to self-pity, depression, and hopelessness. God may have nominated them for a more exalted rank in His future kingdom than can be attained without the apprenticeship in suffering which produces a purer and loftier love. Instead of relapsing into discouragement, resentment, and defeat — *which is a waste of their sorrows* — it is their privilege to take advantage of their suffering and cause it to "work for them." The Apostle Paul says that if one accepts it as from the Lord and rejoices in the suffering, it will be transmuted into eternal glory out of all comparison with the light and temporary affliction (Rom. 5:3 and 2 Cor. 4:17). *Those who are not healed may not need to accept second class citizenship after all, but may be nominated for enhanced rank and eternal glory.*

Our Times Are in God's Hands — Not Satan's
(Psalm 31:15)

There is nothing accidental in the life of an obedient child of God. All born-again believers are in training for rulership. God Himself is personally supervising the training of His Son's Eternal Companion who is to be His governing elite following the Marriage Supper of the Lamb. ''The hands that were pierced do move the wheels of human history and mold the circumstances of individual lives'' (Maclaren).

> My times are in Thy hand:
> My God, I wish them there;
> My life, my friends, my soul I leave
> Entirely to Thy care.
>
> My times are in Thy hand:
> Why should I doubt or fear?
> My Father's hand will never cause
> His child a needless tear.
>
> — William F. Lloyd

A Need-be for Each Pain

God Himself specifically chooses the tools and instruments which He knows are needed to fashion and qualify His Bride for the unique sphere of her operation and service in the eternal kingdom. Someone has said that the turning lathe that has the sharpest knives produces the finest work. When God makes a saint, He uses the sharpest knives on His turning lathe as well. He cannot shape one without pain, but He never uses needless pain. All is chosen in relationship to one's eternal vocation. In some overwhelming catastrophe one may be tempted to say, ''Lord, anything but this.'' An unknown writer explains it thus:

No chance hath brought this ill to me;
'Tis God's own hand, so let it be.
He seeth what I cannot see —
There is a need-be for each pain,
And He one day will make it plain
That earthly loss is heavenly gain.
Like a piece of tapestry
Viewed from the back appears to be
Naught but threads tangled hopelessly;
But in the front a picture rare
Rewards the worker for his care,
Proving his skill and patience rare.
Thou art the Workman, I the frame,
Lord, for the glory of Thy Name,
Perfect Thine image in the same.

This Thing Is From Me

Laura A. Barter Snow has beautifully amplified this truth in her comments on 1 Kings 12:24, in the tract "This Thing Is From Me."

My child, I have a message for you today; let Me whisper it in your ear, that it may gild with glory any storm clouds that may arise, and smooth the rough places upon which you may have to tread. It is short, only five words, but let them sink into your inmost soul; use them as a pillow upon which to rest your weary head: *"This thing is from me."*

Have you ever thought of it, that all that concerns you concerns Me too? For, "He that toucheth you toucheth the apple of mine eye" (Zech. 2:8). "You are very precious in my sight" (Isa. 43:4). Therefore, it is My special delight to educate you.

I would have you learn when temptations assail you, and the "enemy comes in like a flood," that this thing is from Me, that your weakness needs My might, and your safety lies in letting Me fight for you.

Are you in difficult circumstances, surrounded by people who do not understand you, who never consult your taste, who put you in the background? This thing is from Me. I am the God of circumstances. Thou camest not to thy place by accident, it is the very place God meant for thee.

Have you not asked to be made humble? See then, I have placed you in the very school where the lesson is taught; your surroundings and companions are only working out My will.

Are you in money difficulties? Is it hard to make both ends meet? This thing is from Me, for I am your purse-bearer and would have you draw from and depend upon Me. My supplies are limitless (Phil. 4:19). I would have you prove My promises. Let it not be said of you, "In this thing you did not believe the Lord your God" (Deut. 1:32).

Are you passing through a night of sorrow? This thing is from Me. I am the "Man of sorrows and acquainted with grief." I have let earthly comforters fail you, that by turning to Me you may obtain everlasting consolation (2 Thess. 2:16-17). Have you longed to do some great work for Me and instead been laid aside on a bed of pain and weakness? This thing is from Me. I could not get your attention in your busy days and I want to teach you some of My deepest lessons. "They also serve who only stand and wait." Some of My greatest workers are those shut out from active service, that they may learn to wield the weapon of all prayer.

This day I place in your hand this pot of holy oil. Make use of it freely, my child. Let every circumstance that arises, every word that pains you, every interruption that would make you impatient, every revelation of your weakness be anointed with it. The sting will go as you learn to see *Me* in all things.

God's Full-time Occupation

There is no sense to sentiments like these unless God is working in us for eternity. Except for the preparation of her many-mansioned home (John 14:2-3), training the Bride for the throne is His sole occupation. No other cosmology makes sense or harmonizes with the Word (Rom. 8:28). According to this cosmology all that God has done from all eternity and all that He is doing now throughout His infinite domain is related to the preparation of the Bride for her heavenly role. [1] *Preparing the kingdom for her and her for the kingdom is His full-time occupation.* All that He does until the Marriage Supper of the Lamb is concentrated upon this.

Everything which is permitted to come to any member of the Bridehood has been thoroughly thought out. "And he has showered down upon us the richness of his grace — for how well he understands us and knows what is best for us at all times" (Eph. 1:8 *LB*). Thus, when sorrow or suffering come, one may know that it is not accidental or uncontrolled. It is meant to be that way and is intended for one's eternal welfare, promotion, and glory.

The High Rank of the Redeemed

It is easy to doubt the cosmology that holds that the ultimate goal of the universe is the Church. It is easy to question the surpassing importance to God of *one* of His children. In order for one to understand God's supreme interest in him personally, he must remember that redeemed humanity is the highest order of beings in the universe next to the Trinity. The proof of this is that every born-again person is a generic member of the family of God. [2]

Through the new birth we become bona fide members of the original cosmic family (Eph. 3:15), actual generated sons of God (1 John 3:2), "partakers of the divine nature'' (2 Peter 1:4), begotten by Him, impregnated with His "genes", * called the "seed" or "sperma" of God (1 John 5:1, 18 and 1 Peter 1:3, 23), and bearing His heredity. Thus, through the new birth — and I speak reverently — we become the "next of kin" to the Trinity, a kind of extension of the Godhead. . . . Here is a completely new, unique, and exclusive order of beings which may be called a "new species." *There is nothing like it in all the kingdoms of infinity.*[3]

All other orders of beings in the universe are created only. Redeemed humanity is both created and generated.

The Only Valid Explanation of the Universe

When a born-again person understands who he is and what God's purpose for him is, then he can better comprehend why God takes such infinite pains with him. He is God's very own beloved child (1 John 3:2). The Father's mercies are over all of His creation from highest to lowest. His love embraces all, from the tiniest insect which basks in the sunlight for a few brief hours and vanishes forever, to the highest archangel in the blazing glory of the vaulted heavens. But only redeemed humanity are members of God's own household and family (Eph. 2:19). *This is the reason why His care is so minute that the very hairs of one's head are numbered.* This, and this alone, explains the universe. It is the only cosmology that makes sense. *All of the vast physical universe with its countless rolling orbs is not intrinsically important. All derive their value from their relationship to God's plan and purpose for His generic family.* Because it is related to a redeemed personality, a single hair of the head of one of His children concerns Him more than the multiplied galactic systems

---

* No physical relationship is implied.

with their blazing suns, moons, and planets as they pile the heavens and ride their orbits in outer space.

Not Fantasy

Whatever God does, anywhere in His infinite universe, is not done merely as a manifestation of His power, nor for the sake of the inhabitants of outer space, nor for the angelic hosts, but for the sake of His very own generic family, members of His own household. If He creates a new galaxy, it is for their sake. If He originates a new order of angelic beings, it is for them (Heb. 1:14). When He laid down His life on Calvary, it was not for angels or archangels, cherubim or seraphim, nor for any of the other inhabitants of the unseen world, but for human beings made in His own image, who will constitute His Bride. "Consider the incredible love that the Father has shown us in allowing us to be called 'children of God' — and that is not just what we are called, *but what we are.* Our heredity on the Godward side is no mere figure of speech" (1 John 3:1 *Phillips*).

A Mind-boggling Cosmology

This cosmology boggles the human mind — but unless the words of Scripture are meaningless, it is the only valid explanation of the universe. "Eye hath not seen, nor ear heard, neither have entered into the heart of man, the things which God hath prepared for them that love him" (1 Cor. 2:9). Only the Spirit who "searcheth all things, yea, the deep things of God" (1 Cor. 2:10) can make this meaningful. When one realizes, even faintly, who he is; and knows that all that comes to him, whether of weal or woe, is merely God's way of preparing him for royalty as the "elite of the elite" in the future social order; and that the more severe the discipline, the higher his eternal rank — then he can, with the Apostle Paul, "Thank God always for all things" and glory in the tribulation that is creating for him "a far more exceeding and eternal weight of glory." *Only this faith can save one from wasting his sorrows.*

God's Method of Teaching Agape Love

It was this kind of faith that inspired J. R. Miller to write: "Whole, unbruised, unbroken men are of little use to God." They are of little use *because they are deficient in agape love.* Miller says that agape love has to be *learned* — and *that* is the great business of life. It *is* the great business of life because the law of love is the supreme law of eternity. But this love has to be learned within the confines of time and only upon this earth in an environment just like it affords. All the circumstances of this life are arranged for this one purpose: to enable one to learn agape love in order to be qualified to administer the law of love in eternity. Natural affection does not have to be learned but agape love is learned only by being utterly broken, by suffering without resentment. H. E. H. King has beautifully voiced this faith in the following lines:

Here and here alone,
Is given thee to suffer for God's sake;
In other worlds we shall more perfectly
Serve Him and love Him, praise Him, work for Him,
Grow near and nearer Him with all delight,
But then we shall not any more be called
To suffer, which is our appointment here.
Canst thou not suffer, then, one hour or two?

If He should call thee from thy cross today,
Saying, "It is finished — that hard cross of thine,
From which thou prayest for deliverance."
Thinkest thou not some passion of regret
Would overcome thee? Thou wouldst say, "So soon?
Let me go back and suffer yet a while
More patiently — I have not yet praised God."

NOTES

1. See Billheimer, *Destined for the Throne*, chapter 1.
2. See *ibid.*, chapter 2.
3. *Ibid.*, p. 35.

8

THE GREAT BUSINESS OF LIFE —
LEARNING AGAPE LOVE (Continued)

"The Lame Take the Prey"

It is not generally known that George D. Watson, a leader in the early holiness movement, suffered a devastating lapse in his early ministry. Years later, after this disaster had done its work of purging and purifying in his life, he said that God uses for His glory those people and things which are most perfectly broken . . . . Those who are broken in wealth, broken in self-will, broken in their ambitions, broken in their beautiful ideals, broken in worldly reputation, broken in their affections, broken oft-times in health, those who are despised and seem utterly forlorn and helpless, these are the ones the Holy Ghost is seizing upon and using for God's glory. "The lame take the prey" (Isa. 33:23c).

Henry Ward Beecher, who reportedly also suffered a similar catastrophe in his life, said, "Do not be afraid to suffer. Do not be afraid to be overthrown. It is by being cast down and not destroyed; it is by being shaken to pieces, and the pieces torn to shreds, that men become men of might, and that one a host."

Measure thy life by loss and not by gain
Not by the wine drunk, but by the wine poured forth.

For love's strength standeth in love's sacrifice,
And he who suffers most has most to give.

Time — The Vestibule of Eternity

This is utterly contrary to modern psychology. It makes
no sense apart from the Apostle Paul's cosmology which
understands that the unseen is the real and that time is only
the vestibule of eternity. According to modern psychology
a robust ego is necessary for success in an egocentric world.
*But in that social order which is the wave of the future, the
law of love, of self-forgetfulness and selflessness, is
supreme.*

To function in that social order one must be
decentralized. This requires brokenness, which, properly
accepted, secures utter deliverance from self-regard and is
the basis of agape love. *Calvary love, the love that took
Christ to the cross, is the supreme qualification for
rulership in the new order of things to come.* That quality
of love is learned only in time and in a fallen world, as one
yields to be broken. *The full-time occupation of the
enthroned Bride will be expressing God's love-nature
throughout the universe unto the ages of the ages.*

The Broken Violin

The principle, value, and use of brokenness even in this
present order of things is illustrated by J. R. Miller in one
of his books. He tells of a world famous violinist who hired
the services of the most renowned violin maker of his day.
At the time appointed, the violinist returned to take
delivery of the instrument he had authorized. Taking it in
his hands, he skillfully drew the bow across the strings.
Great disappointment swept his face. The quality of tone
did not satisfy his artistic ear. Raising the violin over his
head, he smashed it in pieces on the table, paid the agreed
price, and left.

After a period of time the artist again visited the violin maker. Picking up a violin that was lying on the table, once again he drew the bow across the strings. This time he was charmed by the ravishing beauty of the tone. With astonishment he learned that this was the same violin he had broken to bits. The violin maker had painstakingly gathered up the pieces of the shattered instrument and, skillfully assembling them, had made again the broken violin. Now, the beauty and brilliance of its tone met the exacting demands of the artist's ear.

What Is Meant by Brokenness?

One is not broken until all resentment and rebellion against God and man is removed. One who resents, takes offense, or retaliates against criticism and opposition or lack of appreciation is unbroken. All self-justification and self-defense betrays an unbroken spirit. All discontent and irritation with providential circumstances and situations reveals unbrokenness. Genuine brokenness usually requires years of crushing, heartache, and sorrow. Thus are self-will surrendered and deep degrees of yieldedness and submission developed, without which there is little agape love.

Brokenness also Means Emptiness

Watchman Nee has said that God's great purpose in His dealing with us is to reduce us. This is because any confidence in one's own flesh is fatal to confidence and faith in God. Therefore, before God can release His own power to meet one's crisis need, He must bring that person to the end of himself.

Until one is broken, he is full of himself, his plans, his ambitions, his value judgments. One is often so full of self that there is little room for more of God. Where this is true, God cannot enter in a deeper reality until there has been a divesting of selfish aims and goals, an utter self-emptying. Usually this requires disastrous failures, being "battered with the shocks of doom," complete disillusionment with one's flesh.

> If thou couldst empty all thyself of self.
> Like to a shell dishabited;
> There might He find thee on the ocean shelf,
> And say, "This is not dead,"
> And fill thee with Himself instead.
>
> But thou art all replete with very thou,
> And hast such shrewd activity,
> That when He comes, He says, "This is enow
> Unto itself; 'twere best let it be;
> It is so small and full, there is no room for Me."[1]

A Deeper Death to Self

Further illumination comes from George D. Watson's *A Deeper Death to Self:*

> There is not only a death to sin, but in a great many things there is a deeper death to self — a crucifixion in detail, and in the minutia of life — after the soul has been sanctified. This deeper crucifixion to self is the unfolding and application of all the principles of self-renunciation which the soul agreed to in its full consecration. Job was a perfect man and dead to all sin; but in his great sufferings, he died to his own religious life; died to his domestic affections; died to his theology; all his views of God's providence; he died to a great many things which in themselves were not sin, but which hindered his largest union with God.
>
> Peter, after being sanctified and filled with the Spirit, needed a special vision from heaven to kill him to his traditional theology and Jewish high churchism. *The very largest degrees of self-renunciation, crucifixion,*

and abandonment to God, take place AFTER the work of heart purity. [Emphasis mine.] There are a multitude of things which are not sinful; nevertheless our attachment to them prevents our greatest fulness of the Holy Spirit and our amplest co-operation with God. Infinite wisdom takes us in hand, and arranges to lead us through deep, interior crucifixion to our fine parts, our lofty reason, our brightest hopes, our cherished affections, our religious views, our dearest friendships, our pious zeal, our spiritual impetuosity, our narrow culture, our creeds and churchism, our success, our religious experiences, our spiritual comforts; the crucifixion goes on until we are dead and detached from all creatures, all saints, all thoughts, all hopes, all plans, all tender heart yearnings, all preferences; dead to all troubles, all sorrows, all disappointments; equally dead to all praise or blame, success or failure, comforts or annoyances; dead to all climates and nationalities; dead to all desires but for *Himself*. There are innumerable degrees of interior crucifixion in these various lines. Perhaps not one sanctified person in ten thousand ever reaches that degree of death to self that Paul and Madame Guyon and similar saints have reached.

In contradistinction to heart cleansing, this finer crucifixion of self is gradual; it extends through months and years; the interior spirit is mortified over and over on the same points, till it reaches a state of divine indifference to it. A great host of believers have obtained heart purity, and yet for a long time have gone through all sorts of ''dying daily'' to self, before they found that calm, fixed union with the Holy Ghost which is the deep longing of the child of God. Again in contradistinction to heart cleansing, which is by faith, *this deeper death to self is by suffering.* [Emphasis mine.] This is abundantly taught in Scripture, and confirmed by the furnace experiences of thousands.

Joseph was a sanctified man before being cast into

prison; but there the iron entered into his soul (see Psalm 105:18, margin), and by suffering he reached the highest death of self. There are literally scores of Scripture passages like Psalm 71:19-21, teaching that the upper ranges in the sanctified state are wrought out through suffering. Perhaps the most remarkable passage of the Word on this subject is in Romans, fifth chapter; the first verse teaches justification by faith, the second verse teaches full salvation by faith, and verses three to five teach a deeper death and fuller Holy Ghost life by tribulation.

When the soul undergoes this deeper death of self, it enters into a great wideness of spiritual comprehension and love; a state of almost uninterrupted prayer, of boundless charity for all people; of unutterable tenderness and broadness of sympathy; of deep, quiet thoughtfulness; of extreme simplicity of life and manners; and of deep visions into God and the coming ages. In this state of utter death to self, suffering, sorrow, pain and mortification of all kinds are looked upon with a calm, sweet indifference. Such a soul looks back over its heartbreaking trials, its scalding tears, its mysterious tribulations, with gentle subduedness, without regret, for it now sees God in every step of the way. Into such a soul the Holy Spirit pours the ocean current of His own life; its great work henceforth is to watch the monitions and movements of the Spirit within it, and to yield prompt, loving, unquestioning cooperation with Him. Such a soul has at last, in deed and in truth, reached the place where there is "none of self and all of Thee."

Explanation of the Mystery of Suffering

It is true that "whole, unbruised, unbroken men are of little use to God." In the here and now He cannot greatly use those who are hard, unloving, and self-centered. *But God is not interested in brokenness primarily for its temporal value, great as that may be.* His Bride-elect is in training for the throne. She is in the school of suffering to learn agape love to qualify her for rulership in an economy where the law of love is supreme. This is why God is willing to take a lifetime to teach her love. No other cosmology can explain the mystery of suffering to which Peter says we are called. "Servants, be subject to your masters with all fear; not only to the good and gentle, but also to the froward. For this is thankworthy, if a man for conscience toward God endure grief, suffering wrongfully. For what glory is it, if, when ye be buffeted for your faults, ye shall take it patiently? but if, when ye do well, and suffer for it, ye take it patiently, this is acceptable with God. *For even hereunto were ye called:* because Christ also suffered for us, leaving us an example, that ye should follow his steps" (1 Peter 2:18-21).

Suffering — God's Grand Strategy

Although brokenness is important in God's service upon earth, God's primary purpose in permitting it is to get one prepared for his eternal assignment. *The center of gravity of God's discipline is not time but eternity.* Allowing God's discipline to wean one from vain ambition and selfishness increases agape love and transmutes one's brokenness into eternal glory. Rejecting and refusing the painful circumstances which God planned should crucify all the life of nature and of self *is to waste one's sorrows.*

All the unspeakable suffering of the saints, the combined sorrows, tragedies, heartaches, disappointments, the persecutions and martyrdoms in the history of the Church Universal from the first century to this present throbbing moment, all of these can be justified only by taking eternity into consideration. All of them serve a purpose in the here and now, but their principal design is to teach agape love in preparation for eternal rulership. *Suffering is God's grand strategy for creating rank in the Bridehood for His eternal enterprise.* It seems that only this can possibly justify earth's flood of sorrow. This illuminates Paul's statement to the Philippians: "For unto you it is given in the behalf of Christ, not only to believe on him, but also to suffer for his sake" (Phil. 1:29). Also the statements of Peter: "Beloved, think it not strange concerning the fiery trial which is to try you, as though some strange thing happened unto you: but rejoice, inasmuch as ye are partakers of Christ's sufferings; that, when his glory shall be revealed, ye may be glad also with exceeding joy. If ye be reproached for the name of Christ, happy are ye; for the spirit of glory [lofty rank] and of God resteth upon you" (1 Peter 4:12-14). "But the God of all grace, who hath called us unto his eternal glory by Christ Jesus, after that ye have suffered a while, make you perfect, stablish, strengthen, settle you" (1 Peter 5:10). It should also illuminate Paul's letter to the Thessalonians: "So that we ourselves glory in you in the churches of God for your patience and faith in all your persecutions and tribulations that ye endure: which is a manifest token of the righteous judgment of God, *that ye may be counted worthy of the kingdom of God, for which ye also suffer*" (2 Thess. 1:4-5).

Qualified Through Suffering

In the Philippian passage above, Paul indicates that it is a privilege to suffer for Christ. This is difficult to understand apart from God's eternal purpose for us. While suffering may bear rich fruit in this life, that fruit is not always apparent and much of the time it seems insufficient to justify the suffering. If, as Paul implies, it is a privilege to suffer for Christ, *it must be related to the future order of things.* If God's purpose in keeping a school of suffering here for His children is that of maturing them in agape love in preparation for rulership, then Paul's teaching that suffering is a privilege is rational. This also interprets his word to the Thessalonians concerning their persecutions and afflictions, which afflictions, he says, are "a manifest token of the righteous judgment of God." Why? *"That ye may be counted worthy of the kingdom of God for which ye also suffer."* Paul is saying that without these persecutions and afflictions they could not qualify as meriting their rulership rank. This same concept also interprets and makes rational Peter's exhortation to rejoice as "partakers of Christ's sufferings, that, when his glory shall be revealed, ye may be glad also with exceeding joy . . . for the Spirit of glory and of God resteth upon you" (*New Scofield*). *There is simply no way to explain the Biblical teaching on the glory of suffering and tribulation, except as an apprenticeship for the throne. No love without suffering. No rulership without love. Therefore, ONLY if we suffer shall we reign with Him.*

It is easy to doubt that one's present particular suffering qualifies to serve this high purpose. It may be of such a nature as to tempt one to except it and to feel that it is useless or worse. Some day one may come to understand that the very sorrow which he thought most irrelevant was the one God used for His most glorious ends. This and this alone makes sense of the following lines:

> Things that hurt and things that mar
> Shape the man for perfect praise;
> Shock and strain and ruin are
> Friendlier than smiling days.

Solomon's Temple

This principle is illustrated in the building of Solomon's Temple. Every stone that went into that amazing structure was hewn to such exact specifications at the quarry site that each stone fitted perfectly into the place for which it was designed. "And the house, when it was in building, was built of stone made ready before it was brought thither: so that there was neither hammer nor axe nor any tool of iron heard in the house, while it was in building'' (1 Kings 6:7).

Believers Are Living Stones

A. N. Hodgkin, in *Christ in All the Scriptures,* says, ''All true believers in all ages are the living stones in that heavenly Temple, and God is preparing them in His quarry down here, amid the noise and tumult of earth, each for his place in His Temple above. Rugged and shapeless are the stones to begin with; no wonder that the blows of the hammer fall heavily, that the chisel is sharp, and the polishing severe before the stones are ready.''[2]

At present we are not what we should be, neither are we what we shall be. But God does not work without a pattern or design. He knows what He is doing. There is nothing accidental about the providences that come into our lives. There is a Hand that is guiding and controlling these providences. There is a purpose running through all the events and circumstances. This purpose may not be evident to us, but there is an eye that always watches the pattern. It is God who fashions us.

> 'Tis the Master who holds the mallet,
>   And day by day
> He is chipping whatever environs
>   The form away;
> Which, under His skillful cutting,
>   He means shall be
> Wrought silently out to beauty
>   Of such degree
> Of faultless and full perfection,
>   That angel eyes
> Shall look on the finished labor
>   With new surprise,
> That even His boundless patience

Could grave His own
Features upon such fractured
And stubborn stone.

The Shaping of the Stones

Hodgkin points out that when they are removed from the quarry, the stones are rugged and shapeless. Quarry stones are insensitive but the "living stones" with which God is working are not. This means that God cannot shape without pain. *Where there is no pain, no shaping is achieved.* The tools He must use are sharp and abrasive. Quarry stones cannot resist but the "living stones" may. When they do, *their sorrow and pain is wasted.* If God cannot shape one for his distinctive place in eternity without the use of affliction, may this not explain why many people continue to suffer physical illness in spite of long continued prayer for healing? If character is God's supreme aim in the universe and if character cannot be developed without pain, does this not illuminate the passage: "Whom the Lord loveth he chasteneth"? (Heb. 12:6). Maybe God just cannot get that special stone He needs for a particular place any other way. If so, is He to be denied, and are the person's sorrows wasted if he eventually qualifies for his unique place in that ethereal structure?

NOTES

1. J. R. Miller, *When the Song Begins*, p. 39.
2. A. N. Hodgkin, *Christ in All the Scriptures* (Glasgow: Pickering & Inglis, 1908), pp. 86-87.

9

LEARNING AGAPE LOVE THROUGH FAMILY RELATIONSHIPS

According to our thesis, life is intended to be an education in agape love. All circumstances, whether of joy or sorrow, which are permitted to come to a child of God are for the purpose of teaching and maturing him in the love which is the prerequisite for rulership in the ultimate economy of God. This world is a laboratory in which those destined for the throne are learning by actual practice to be governed by the law of love, which principle they will administer in the ultimate social order.

Earth, the Sphere of Learning Love

There is only one place and time in which agape love can be learned and that is in the here and now, in a world just like this one. As C. S. Lovett points out in a recent book, [1] this character of agape love could not be produced in heaven. This is rather a startling statement, but he says that "Heaven is no place to raise kids." There is no way to produce godliness there. The conditions required to bring people to spiritual maturity are not found there.

Superficially, one would think that heaven would be the ideal place to produce godly character. No more suffering, sorrow, crying, nor pain (Rev. 21:4). "No more foes to make afraid." But, as Lovett points out, this means no more tension or strain. No more tests or temptations. No more opposition or hindrances. Total relaxation. Would not this kind of milieu, this kind of environment, this kind of surroundings, be ideal for the production of heavenly character? The answer is: *By no means.* Dr. Lovett asks: "What happens to children when all stresses are taken away? What happens when they are shielded from hardship, stresses, and oppositions of life? Do they grow, or merely stagnate?"

You know that is no way to bring about strength of character. Therefore, heaven is no place to *bring* sons to maturity. *That* must be done here on earth in just the kind of a world God has placed us in. Lovett says, "A coddled child is frightful." And you know that a coddled saint is impossible.

Does this mean there will be no growth in heaven? Indeed not. There the redeemed will live in an *entirely new order* (Rev. 21:4-5). In that order there may be many other stimulants to growth, and one of them will be praise and worship. Heaven is one grand paean of praise. In worship and praise of the infinitely lovely God one exercises the most sublime and divine dimensions of the human character. In this exercise, all of the most transcendent, ineffable, and Godlike qualities of the being are activated and therefore enlarged. This growth process will be eternally accelerated in the celestial atmosphere and practice of praise and worship. There will be no need there for the stimulus of earthly sorrow, stress, and pain.

Purity — Instantaneous

A person receives purity of heart by an instantaneous act of faith in receiving the filling with the Holy Spirit (Acts 15:7-9; see also Acts 10:44-47). But maturity in agape love is another thing. Without purity of heart maturity is impossible. Even with purity of heart, maturity is an extended process impossible apart from tribulation, pain, and stress. There is no shortcut. After many years, the Apostle Paul testified that he had not yet attained the summit of maturity (Phil. 3:12-14).

Maturity — A Lifetime Process

Maturing into advanced states of Christian character and agape love is, of necessity, a lifetime operation. Take for example the grace of long-suffering. How is it acquired? Lovett answers: "By suffering a long time." But there is no suffering in heaven. Therefore, long-suffering cannot be acquired there.

What about patience? In my youth, some preachers of my acquaintance implied that the crisis experience of holiness brought instant patience, like instant coffee, instant grits, or other instant foods. But how are instant foods produced? By precooking. They require the application of heat or pressure or both. It is the same with patience. There is no such thing as instant grits or instant patience. Advanced degrees of patience (which is only a by-product or manifestation of agape love) are gained by enduring one anxiety after another. But there is no anxiety in heaven, therefore patience cannot be learned there.

Consider the grace of forgiveness, another manifestation of agape love. Does one not have to be hurt or offended before he can forgive? Then high degrees of the grace of forgiveness are developed only by being hurt again and again and again. But there are no hurts or offenses in heaven, so forgiveness cannot be learned there.

Life — A Laboratory

Therefore a lifetime of sorrows, anguish, and disappointments is required to transform one into the lofty likeness of the Lord, to lead him into advanced degrees of maturity in Christlikeness and agape love. And these things are not found in heaven. Earth alone provides the kind of situations that produce mature sainthood. Here and here alone can one be tested by sorrow, frustration, and life-changing stresses. It is important to remember that this life is a laboratory, an apprenticeship in which God is teaching His children agape love in preparation for rulership.

Home — A Microcosm

The home is the logical place to begin a course in learning agape love. As Dr. Lovett has said, "Marriage and the home is the center of all life on earth. . . . It is a complete laboratory with all of the stresses and strains, trials and pressures packed under one roof. . . . Everything needed to produce Christlikeness in us can be found in the home." In other words, the home is a microcosm or miniature world, a facsimile of the world at large. The home, with its environment of stress and strain, is the best place to learn agape love. That is one of the reasons why God ordained the home, why He "set the solitary in families" (Psalm 68:6). Lovett has said, "Marriage is the most stressful fact of life. If the whole of life is stress, then marriage is the center of stress."

Newlyweds Often Self-centered

J. R. Miller has said

No two lives, however thorough their former acquaintance may have been, however long they may have moved together in society or mingled in the closer and more intimate relations of a ripening friendship, ever find themselves perfectly in harmony on their marriage day. It is only when that mysterious blending begins after marriage which no language can explain that each finds so much in the other that was never discovered before. . . . There are incompatibilities that were never dreamed of till they were revealed in the attrition of domestic life. [2]

There may be exceptions, but most newlyweds have not

yet learned the true meaning of unselfishness. They may be saved, sanctified or filled with the Holy Spirit, and still be unconsciously self-centered. One of God's main purposes in ordaining marriage and the home is not primarily for pleasure, as is ordinarily supposed, but to decentralize the self, to teach agape love. The stresses of marriage and the home are designed to produce brokenness, to wean one from self-centeredness, and to produce the graces of sacrificial love and gentleness.

Because so few people understand the nature and purpose of marriage, when unexpected stresses and strains develop they are tempted to feel that they have made a mistake and perhaps have married the wrong person. The next step is to seek a way of escape by one means or another, sometimes through a professional marriage counselor or, more often, the divorce court.

A Spiritual Problem

If the marriage counselor is a professional and works for pay, his services, based as they are on Freudian principles, are probably worthless or worse. Except where there is organic difficulty, the root of all conflicts in the home is not mental but spiritual. Psychology and psychiatry are usually totally irrelevant. *A spiritual problem always has a spiritual cause and requires a spiritual solution.* Many counselors, even some who are Christians, have been so influenced by Freud that they are totally unprepared to deal with a spiritual problem in a scriptural way. Many spiritually discerning persons are quite convinced that psychiatry is Satan's substitute for the Biblical remedy for disturbed relations. Many psychiatrists seek to help the person under stress by relieving him of personal responsibility for his difficulty — which only compounds the trouble. The origin of the conflict, except in organic cases, is almost invariably spiritual. The ego is inflated. Love is lacking. This is entirely a spiritual problem. The way out is *not* through separation or divorce. That would frustrate God's purpose and only aggravate the problems.

Learning Sacrificial Love

If one or both of the persons involved is born again, God's design is that each shall teach the other agape love. And this is not easy. The life of nature and of self dies hard. But if even one partner understands that life is for learning love and that the home is the arena where it is best taught and learned, a beginning in decentralization may be made. If the couple can comprehend that neither life nor marriage is made primarily for pleasure but for learning sacrificial love, *they may not waste their sorrows.*

Horizontal Versus Vertical

Trouble in a horizontal relationship is always the result of trouble in the vertical relationship — with God. Somewhere self-will has taken over. *Antagonism toward a mate is first of all antagonism toward God. Lack of love for a marriage partner is really lack of love for God.* "Beloved, let us love one another: for love is of God; and every one that loveth is born of God and knoweth God. He that loveth not knoweth not God. . . . If we love one another, God dwelleth in us, and his love is perfected in us. . . . If a man say, I love God, and hateth his brother [or mate], he is a liar: for he that loveth not his brother [or mate] whom he hath seen, how can he love God whom he hath not seen?" (1 John 4:7-8, 12, 20).

The Right to Surrender Rights

When either marriage partner gives as the excuse for separation that love for the other person is gone, the trouble is not primarily between the couple themselves but between one or both of them and God. When at least one of them gets really right with God, he no longer stubbornly insists on his rights or having things his way. Someone has said that the only right a Christian has is the right to give up his rights. This agrees with the Sermon on the Mount, Matthew chapters five and six. *The partner closest to God will almost always be the first to yield.* Love for God will enable him to surrender his prerogatives and accept self-crucifixion. If he or she is not willing to do this, it is because his love for God is deficient. Refusal to suffer loss for Christ's sake is really rebellion against God.

Repentance and Restitution

If this is the situation, no amount of professional counseling or psychiatric treatment will change it until the spiritual problem is solved. It is doubtful if a paid counselor or psychiatrist understands this and can be of any help. Help will come only when one or both of the partners understands that life is for learning agape love in preparation for rulership in eternity and is willing to suffer the pain involved in adjustment and forgiveness. Repentance toward God for all unlovingness and restitution toward one another will bring the growth in love that God intends. Paul gives instruction in Ephesians 5:21-23 concerning submission which is so vital to growth in love: "Submit yourselves one to another in the fear of God. Wives, submit yourselves unto your own husbands, as unto the Lord. For the husband is the head of the wife, even as Christ is the head of the church; and he is the saviour of the body." Peter, also, emphasizes this principle in 1 Peter 5:5-6, "Likewise, ye younger, submit yourselves unto the elder. Yea, all of you be subject one to another, and be clothed with humility: for God resisteth the proud, and giveth grace to the humble. Humble yourselves therefore under the mighty hand of God, *that he may exalt you in due time.*" Unwillingness to accept these principles of submission will result not only in increased heartache and pain, *but in wasting one's sorrows.*

An Insecure Foundation

Much marriage counseling is oriented toward the here and now. The primary goal is to heal the endangered marriage in the interest of the present happiness of the partners. This is very natural. But so long as the pair suffers with the illusion that the main purpose of life and wedlock is blissful pleasure and happiness, the foundation of their marriage is insecure. Until they understand that life and marriage is an apprenticeship for the practice of agape love in preparation for rulership where the law of love is supreme, they are in danger of eternal loss. If they spend their years in regrets, disappointments, and recriminations *they have wasted their sorrows.* If they accept one another as God's disciplinary agents to bring each other into increasing selflessness and growing agape love, they may not only find greater happiness here but achieve a "far more exceeding and eternal weight of glory" in the afterward.

A Tragedy of Our Times

All of the efforts by psychologists and psychiatrists to bring about a reorientation and reintegration of personalities in marriage without dealing with the basic spiritual problem are in vain. It is sad to see the Church and the ministry forsaking the Biblical way of soul healing for a massive satanic delusion. It is one of the most lamentable tragedies of recent history. "Be astonished, O ye heavens, at this, and be horribly afraid, be ye very desolate, saith the Lord. For my people have committed two evils: they have forsaken me the fountain of living waters, and hewed them out cisterns, broken cisterns, that can hold no water" (Jer. 2:12-13). Nowhere is this more true than in the professional mental health programs operated under the supervision of religious groups.

A Professional Opinion

This is the opinion not only of a layman, but of some highly respected professionals. In chapters six and seven of his book *The Crisis in Psychiatry and Religion*,[3] Dr. O. Hobart Mowrer, research psychologist at the University of Illinois and formerly President of the American Psychological Association, has strongly reproved the Christian ministry for referring the mentally disturbed members of their congregations to psychiatrists when the ministers of the Word of God alone have the answers to these kinds of problems.

An Atheistic Philosophy

It is a sorrowful reflection upon Him who said, "Come unto *me,* all ye that labour and are heavy laden, and I will give you rest" (Matt. 11:28), when His servants and representatives become so undiscerning, confused, and powerless as to seek the assistance of a profession which is predominantly atheistic, deterministic, and evolutionary in its philosophy. Furthermore, a large segment of the profession has repudiated Biblical principles of morality, attributing much mental disturbance to over-conscientiousness in efforts to live by those principles.

Seduction as Therapy

An article in *The Atlanta Constitution* for January 26, 1976, reveals the widespread practice by professional counselors of using so-called sexual therapy as a treatment in mental illness. Under the headline "Seduction in Therapy Called a Major Problem" the dispatch reads: "One of the most pressing problems facing the rapidly expanding field of sex therapy today is the practice of therapists who sometimes seduce patients seeking cures to sexual problems. . . ."

A lengthy discussion of sexual relations between therapists and patients was led by Yale University psychiatrist Fritz Redich, who said such sex with clients is frequent among many types of professionals.

In a recent newspaper article, a psychiatrist is quoted as openly admitting this practice and saying that he gets a weekly fee of fifty dollars for his "professional" service in one instance. That makes him a gigolo or male prostitute masquerading as a therapist.

Psychoanalysis Not a Science

Although, according to the above dispatch, the practice is frequent, the charge is not being made here that it is representative of the profession as a whole. While there are some professing Christian psychiatrists, it seems a misnomer to this writer. According to some recognized authorities, psychiatry is no science even though it poses as one. It is called a faith, not logic. [4] While the profession seems to proliferate, some well-known writers call mental health a myth and identify neurosis as "not a medical problem but a moral conflict." [5]

Integrity Therapy

Dr. Mowrer has sponsored a new approach to mental health problems which is called "Integrity Therapy." It boils down to the Biblical method of healing: repentance, restitution, forgiveness, and full transparency with all parties concerned, leading to a right relationship with God and one another. (Integrity Therapy, Room 330, Gregory Hall, Urbana, Ill.) *A right vertical relationship is the secret of a satisfying horizontal relationship. Perfect transparency with God and one another is the remedy for stress in personal relationships.*

A Professional's Advice

Author-psychologist Lee R. Steiner's remarks should give pause to the minister who is, consciously or unconsciously, enamored with the psychiatric approach to mental health and spiritual problems: "It is my impression from twenty years of study of where people take their troubles and why they seek out the sources they do, that the ministry makes a tremendous mistake when it swaps what it has for psychosomatic dressing. Through the ages, ministry has been the force that has at least attempted to keep morality alive. It would be a pity if, in one of the areas of greatest moral crisis, the clergy should suddenly abandon its strength for something that has no validity, no roots, and no value. It is my impression that they would do far better to cling to what they have. Judaism has endured for almost 6,000 years. Christianity for about 2,000. Where will psychoanalysis be 25 years from now? . . . I predict it will take its place along with phrenology and mesmerism."[6]

The Only Remedy

To reemphasize: When a home or marriage is threatened, the basic cause is spiritual. Therefore, the remedy is spiritual, not psychological. Stresses and strains are certain to come. When the parties accept them as God's way of teaching them agape love in preparation for the throne in eternity, welcoming them by offering the sacrifice of praise (Heb. 13:15), domestic conflicts may be resolved and transmuted into future glory.

Marital Unfaithfulness

These are hazardous days in which almost all cherished values are crumbling. The world is adrift in a sea of uncertainty and doubt. Society is in a state of ethical shock. The social order is disintegrating. Moral chaos thrives. Sexual anarchy prevails. Mass insanity threatens. This disintegration of the social order is an evidence of an invasion of sex-oriented demons, driving up the divorce rate and destroying the institution of marriage, the home, and the family. But God can use this very situation to develop agape love in His Bride-elect.

Overruling Moral Failure

One of the greatest opportunities for learning agape love is presented to the Christian man or woman whose mate has become the victim of promiscuous sex demons. There is no greater temptation to bitterness than the unfaithfulness of a marriage partner. Thousands are being caught in this maelstrom of moral permissiveness induced by the "new morality," and the relaxation of moral standards it promotes. Mrs. Billy Graham has been quoted as saying that if God continues to spare our decadent morals, He should apologize to Sodom and Gomorrah. Husbands and wives may not realize it, but this very situation offers an unprecedented opportunity to enhance eternal rank by learning a deeper dimension of agape love. If one succumbs to resentment, self-pity, and revenge, *he has wasted his sorrow.* But if one understands that grace can overrule this sorrow and use it for teaching agape love, he may be able to use his unspeakable anguish for everlasting gain. Not many do, but some have triumphed.

An Affirmation

For those who are having any sort of domestic difficulty, the following affirmation is suggested:

> Father, I offer the sacrifice of praise for my mate just as he (she) is because You have permitted him (her) to be this way and have brought us together in a marriage relationship. I know that You are able and therefore I know that You are working through him (her) as he (she) is, to bring Your purposes to pass, overruling his (her) spiritual, character, and personality limitations for Your glory. Amen.

Try practicing this affirmation at every moment of irritation or injury for six months and see what happens.

The Generation Gap

Although this is the day of the so-called generation gap, it is as old as Adam and his son Cain, and Noah and his son Ham. However, Freudian psychology and the school of psychiatry it spawned has greatly aggravated and enlarged the breach between parents and children. The resulting alienation and the rejection of moral and spiritual ideals by the younger generation is capable of producing the most agonizing suffering. This is a problem of massive proportions. The fact that no parent is perfect and so may be partially responsible for the alienation does not assuage the grief. The wounds opened by filial ingratitude are only aggravated by the blighting effects of this alienation upon the loved one himself, who is dearer than life. King David has many brothers and sisters who join him in his soliloquy over a son who reaped as he sowed, and brought crushing sorrow to his parents. But according to the Apostle Paul, even this devastating grief may be transmuted into a "far more exceeding and eternal weight of glory" if it is allowed to work in the parent that deeper dimension of agape love that is redemptive. Out of the agony of rejection a parent may discover self-centeredness of which he was unaware. By sincere repentance and self-repudiation he may grow in sacrificial love which is both healing, restorative, and eternally rewarding. This may be one reason why God permits the agonies of the generation gap. *The resulting crushing sorrows should not be wasted.* The cost of learning to love may be high, but God considers no price too great. By these sorrows He is training His Bride-elect to live by the law of love.

NOTES

1. C. S. Lovett, *Unequally Yoked Wives* (Baldwin Park, CA: Personal Christianity, 1968). Used by permission.
2. J. R. Miller, *Weekday Religion,* pp. 67-68.
3. O. Hobart Mowrer, *The Crisis in Psychiatry and Religion* (Princeton: D. Van Nostrand Company, Inc., 1961).
4. O. Hobart Mowrer, ed., *Morality and Mental Health* (Chicago: Rand McNally & Company, 1967), p. 56.
5. *Ibid.,* p. 17.
6. *Ibid.,* p. 301.

10

LEARNING AGAPE LOVE THROUGH WRONGFUL SUFFERING

To recapitulate: If all born-again believers are in apprenticeship for rulership, and if a lofty dimension of agape love is the supreme qualification for high rank and authority in that eternal social order toward which the universe is moving, and if a high dimension of agape love cannot be achieved without suffering, could this explain why God permits many who seek healing to suffer on, even for a lifetime?

The Discipline of Delay

If God healed everyone immediately where would be the opportunity for character training? If God delivered everyone from conflict, oppression, and opposition at the first call, where would be the opportunity for the perseverance that creates character? If tribulation were lifted at the first cry, where would be the chance for exercise in patience which issues in heavenly character, the chief ingredient of which is agape love? If Jesus' human experience in leadership could not be perfected without suffering, could our training for heavenly rulership be perfected without it? The answer is: probably not.

How Pure Evil Is Transformed

The question is: How are "these light afflictions which are but for a moment," but which seem unbearable and endless to us, to be transmuted into that "far more exceeding and eternal weight of glory"? *One's afflictions can be made to work for him only by a correct subjective attitude.* To many it is a mystery how a *subjective* attitude toward an *objective* situation can so modify its effect that pure "evil" is transformed into a sublime dimension of "good."

The Eternal Essence of a Situation

Consider the following: *Nothing that can come to one from any source can injure him unless it causes him to have a wrong attitude. It is one's response that blesses or burns.* Amy Carmichael has said that the eternal essence of a thing is not in the thing itself but in one's reaction to it. The distressing situation will pass but one's reaction toward it will leave a moral and spiritual deposit in his character that is eternal. This being true, then all that God permits to come to one must be working for his good unless he allows it to separate him from God. "The only real calamity in life is to lose one's faith in God" (Maclaren). The circumstances and situations which confront one are beyond his control; he can do nothing about them. But with the help of God he can control his reaction, his subjective attitude. *That is entirely within his own jurisdiction.* If, because of the apparent evil that has come, one allows himself to fall into an attitude of self-pity, frustration, and rebellion toward people and God, his character deteriorates and *he is wasting his sorrow.* But when one accepts the advice of the Apostle James, everything is different. "Consider it pure joy, my brothers, whenever you face trials of many kinds, because you know that the testing of your faith develops perseverance. Perseverance must finish its work so that you may be mature and complete, not lacking anything" (James 1:2-4 *NIV*). This is in harmony with Paul's statement in

Romans 5:3-5: "We glory in tribulations also, knowing that tribulation worketh patience; and patience, experience; and experience, hope; and hope maketh not ashamed, because the love of God is shed abroad in our hearts by the Holy Spirit who is given unto us" (*New Scofield*). According to this passage, the ultimate result of rejoicing in tribulation is agape love shed abroad in the heart. This is supreme gain.

Blessed Be Suffering

If God cannot develop the quality of character which is needed for rulership in the ages to come without suffering, then should not one's attitude be, "Blessed be suffering"? *Rank in heaven will be determined not by magnetic personality, glittering talents, towering intellect, or other coveted endowments, but by the depth and quality of one's love.* Earth, with its sorrow, heartbreak, disappointments and pain, is the only place, and this life is the only time, when this love can be developed. *This love is the coin, currency, and legal tender of heaven.* It can be developed only in the school of suffering. Before suffering has done its benevolent work, how hard, harsh, arrogant, cutting, overbearing, tactless, impatient, even churlish, many of us have been. How often we have ridden roughshod over the legitimate feelings, sensibilities, and opinions of others. These are all traits of self-centeredness. Only by suffering, oftentimes severely, are these unlovely characteristics and dispositions softened and sweetened. *This is why God has to take many of us through refining fires, why many must be "battered with the shocks of doom" until they are bruised, broken, and made utterly empty of themselves.* ·

O, to be nothing, nothing,
Only to lie at His feet,
A broken and emptied vessel,
For the Master's use made meet.

Job's Decentralization

Before he suffered, Job knew God by reputation only. Afterward, he said, "Now mine eye seeth thee." Before his suffering was complete he argued with God, actually accusing Him of malfeasance. Read Job chapter ten. Afterward, he said, "I abhor myself, and repent in dust and ashes" (Job 42:6). Job's experience is an illustration of 1 Peter 4:1, "He that hath suffered in the flesh hath ceased from sin." God testified that Job was a holy man, yet there were traits of self-centeredness of which, at first, he was totally unaware and which could be spotlighted and removed only by deep affliction.

The proof that out of Job's long trial of severe sorrow came a new dimension of agape love is the fact that he was willing to pray for his severe critics and they were spared the Lord's judgment. *To accept criticism sweetly, without retaliation or resentment, is an evidence of growth in love.* This is one reason why Jesus said to "love your enemies" — because they afford one the opportunity to grow in agape love, the insignia of rank in eternity (Matt. 5:44-48).

"On-the-job" Training

All of God's discipline and training is directed toward increasing and perfecting one's love. All adversity, of whatever character and magnitude, is permitted for this purpose. God is using one's temporal circumstances, personality clashes, personal hostilities, unjust criticism, financial reverses, poverty, physical affliction, frailty, pain, and even old age as "on-the-job" training for the exercise and development of agape love. This training is not primarily for temporal value and advantage, since life's day is often nearing its end before one learns the deeper lessons of love, but because it is the coin, currency, and legal tender of eternity. We need often to be reminded that we are in apprenticeship here in life's school of suffering to learn love primarily as eternal equipment and qualification for rulership in heaven's ultimate social order.

Furthermore, this means that all hindrance to the believer's deliverance clear up to total glorification is on the human side. One man, Enoch, proved, verified, and confirmed this principle by appropriating faith for glorification (Gen. 5:24 and Heb. 11:5). Enoch's experience proves that there is a legal basis for full deliverance in this life from every result of the Fall for every child of God. *If one fallen man is legally delivered* (see Chapter 4), *then potentially, all must be.* This is the only explanation of Enoch's experience.

Affliction and Character Development

Since Enoch's experience was the result of a perfect faith (Heb. 11:5), all failure to obtain full deliverance from any result of the Fall must be the failure of faith. And failure of faith in well-taught believers is the result of one thing: defects in Christian character. Therefore, all infirmities, sickness, and disease that remain in a knowledgeable believer's life must be related to character development alone. Alexander Maclaren, believing that every affliction comes with a message from the heart of God, said that if we knew ourselves better, and could see as God sees, *we could trace all of our unanswered prayers to defects in our own Christian character.*

Because these things are true, then all afflictions of every kind that are not removed in answer to prayer should be understood as God's way of disciplining character into the pattern of Godlikeness which is fitting one specifically for his particular role in the ages to come.

Purposeful Sorrow

All that God permits to come to the members of His Bridehood here is intended to mature them in love which will be necessary in their administrative capacity as "kings and priests." Repeating: Life on earth in a fallen social order is the only milieu or situation in which this love has any chance for practice and development. This explains why Paul said, "If we suffer, we shall also reign with him" (2 Tim. 2:12) and "If so be that we suffer with him, that we may be also glorified together" (Rom. 8:17).

Purposeful Tribulation

It has been pointed out that as soon as a person is born again he enters apprenticeship for rulership in that social order where the law of agape love is supreme. Since tribulation is necessary for the decentralization of the self and the development of agape love, Paul says we are to glory in it, and only to the extent to which we glory in it does tribulation serve us and achieve God's purpose. If we fight against it by self-pity and rebellion, by murmuring and complaining, by accusing God of malfeasance — that is, not treating one justly — *we are wasting our sorrows.*

Called to Unjust Suffering

None of the things, not even the worst things, that come to a child of God are ever accidental. They are controlled experiments intended to give him opportunity to exercise and learn agape love. No one in his right mind would count it a privilege to suffer wrongfully unless he sees it as an opportunity to increase his rank in the eternal kingdom. God must have had this in mind when He inspired Peter to write: "Slaves, submit yourselves to your masters with all respect, not only to those who are good and considerate, but also to those who are harsh. For it is commendable if a man bears up under the pain of unjust suffering because he is conscious of God. But how is it to your credit if you receive a beating for doing wrong and endure it? But if you suffer for doing good and you endure it, this is commendable before God. *To this you were called,* because Christ suffered for you, leaving you an example, that you should follow in his steps'' (1 Peter 2:18-21 *NIV*). Understanding that this is God's way of enabling one to increase his eternal rank can hold one steady under unjust suffering. May this not explain why God permits persecution and martyrdom behind the Iron Curtain, as well as the injustices and heart-breaking situations which He permits in the lives of all saints everywhere? ''For it has been granted to you on behalf of Christ not only to believe on him, but also to suffer for him'' (Phil. 1:29 *NIV*).

Trouble a Trust

It is difficult to receive injury from others without feeling resentment. It is hard to suffer wrongfully without becoming cynical and bitter. It is a problem to keep love in the heart through all unkindness, ingratitude, misunderstanding, injuries, abuses, and griefs. God may permit great personal inequity to come to one because it is one of the ways agape love can grow and eternal rank be enhanced. Trouble is a trust, and for this reason one should ''Consider it pure joy . . . whenever you face trials of many kinds, because you know that the testing of your faith develops perseverance. Perseverance must finish its work so that you may be mature and complete'' (James 1:2-4 *NIV*). ''In this you greatly rejoice, though now for a little while you may have suffered grief in all kinds of trials. These have come so that your faith — of greater worth than gold, which perishes though refined by fire — may be proved genuine and may result in praise [enhanced rank], glory and honor when Jesus Christ is revealed'' (1 Peter 1:6-7 *NIV*).

A Fertilizer Of Character

Notice that ''trials of many kinds'' issue in maturity (of love), and ''grief in all kinds of trials'' results in ''praise, glory and honor when Jesus Christ is revealed.'' If a child of God could actually see into the future and fully visualize the exalted rank that the school of suffering is creating for him, it would be easier to "glory in tribulation" — which often, instead, immerses him in deep depression. Austin Phelps has said, "Suffering is a wonderful fertilizer to the roots of character [agape love]. This is the only thing we can carry into eternity. . . . To gain the most of it and the best of it, is the object of probation." Cortland Myers has said, "Some day, God is going to reveal the fact to every Christian, that the very principles they now rebel against, have been the instruments He used in perfecting their characters and moulding them into perfection, polished stones for His great building yonder."

If we could push ajar the gates of life,
    And stand within, and all God's working see,
We might interpret all this doubt and strife,
    And for each mystery could find a key.

But not today. Then be content, poor heart;
    God's plans, like lilies pure and white, unfold.
We must not tear the close-shut leaves apart —
    Time will reveal the calyxes of gold.

And if, through patient toil, we reach the land
    Where tired feet, with sandals loosed, may rest,
When we shall clearly know and understand,
    I think that we shall say, "God knew best."

God's Slow Work

In his writing, Dr. J. R. Miller tells of a young mother whose two small children were snatched from her arms by the Grim Reaper in one day. She collapsed under the burden of her grief. One day, through her tears she sobbed, "I don't see why God made me." Her auntie, who was caring for her and was more wise in the ways of the Lord, said, "Dearie, you are not yet made. God is making you now." God takes one as he is and spends a lifetime fashioning him into His image.

> Behind my life the Weaver stands,
>   And works His wondrous will.
> I leave it in His all-wise hands,
>   And trust His perfect skill;
> Should mystery enshroud His plan,
>   And my short sight be dim,
> I will not try the whole to scan,
>   But leave each thread with Him.
>
> Nor till the loom is silent,
>   And the shuttles cease to fly,
> Shall God unfold the pattern,
>   And explain the reason why
> The dark threads were as needful
>   (In the Master's skillful hand)
> As the threads of gold and silver
>   In the pattern which He planned.
>
> — Unknown

This Is Not the Devil's World

"This is not a world of chance — there is no chance anywhere. This is not the devil's world. All the universe is under the Father's personal sway. Our adversary is a created being under God's control. The divine hand is active in all the affairs of earth. 'My Father worketh hitherto and I work.' In all that He permits — joy, sorrow, success, failure, hope and fear, pleasure and pain, He is making us.

"But God does not make us all at once. The process is a long one, running through all the years of life, how many soever those years may be. God begins making us when we are born into the world, and His work in us goes on continuously unto the end of our days. There is never an hour when some new touch is not given to our life, some new line marked in our character. . . . Always God is on the field and He works in and through all experiences. . . . There is nothing accidental in any of the providences that come into our lives.'' [1]

It is important to remember, as Dr. Miller says, that Satan is a created being. He is *not* Lord of the universe, because he is a part of creation. Whatever authority he won through Adam's fall was lost at Calvary. In Matthew 28:18 Jesus said, ''All authority is given unto *me* in heaven and in earth'' (*New Scofield*). Predicated upon the victory of Calvary, in Luke 10:19 Jesus delegated that authority to His disciples and through them to the Church. Until Satan's final incarceration (Rev. 20:10) and the subsequent Marriage Supper of the Lamb, God is using Satan for His own purposes to teach the Bride-elect the technique of overcoming (Rev. 3:21) and a deeper dimension of agape love.

When one understands that agape love is the insignia of rank in that social order called the kingdom of God, and that this love is cultivated only in the school of suffering, he can better appreciate the truth expressed in these lines:

Sometime, when all life's lessons have been learned,
  And sun and stars forevermore have set,
The things which our weak judgments here have spurned,
  The things o'er which we grieved with lashes wet,
Will flash before us, out of life's dark night,
  As stars shine most in deeper tints of blue,
And we shall see how all God's plans were right,
  And what we thought reproof, was love most true.
                     — Unknown

NOTES

1. J. R. Miller, *God's Slow Making of Us.*

11

LEARNING AGAPE LOVE THROUGH LIFE'S FAILURES

No Price Too Great

God will go to any length to mold and mature one in agape love. He considers no price too great because He knows the glory that is ahead.

> When God wants to drill a man,
> And thrill a man,
> And skill a man
> To play the noblest part;
> When He yearns with all His heart
> To create so great and bold a man
> That all the world shall be amazed,
> Watch His methods, watch His ways!
> How He ruthlessly perfects
> Whom He royally elects!
> How He hammers him and hurts him,
> And with mighty blows converts him
> Into trial shapes of clay which
> Only God understands;
> While his tortured heart is crying
> And he lifts beseeching hands!
> How he bends but never breaks
> When his good He undertakes;
> How He uses whom He chooses,

And with every purpose fuses him;
By every act induces him
To try his splendor out —
God knows what He's about.
                              — Angela Morgan (adapted)

The writer of the foregoing lines apparently was thinking mostly of God's training for time. But God's purpose in taking a man through a course of severe discipline as described in this poem is to prepare him for high rank in the eternal kingdom. "For the common deeds of the common day, are ringing bells in the far away," that is, in eternity.

The Tip of the Iceberg

Many excellent writers justify suffering on the basis of its value in time and the contribution it makes to character and the kingdom in the here and now. There is much to be said for this viewpoint. Volumes have been written concerning the value of tribulation and sorrow in the building of character and the fashioning of a meritorious life style. In one of his books, J. R. Miller has expressed this faith beautifully thus: "We do not know how much we owe to suffering. Many of the richest blessings that have come down to us from the past are the fruit of sorrow and pain." [1]

In another place Dr. Miller has said, "The world's greatest blessings have come out of its greatest sorrows. Goethe is reported to have said, 'I never had an affliction which did not turn into a poem.' It is probable that the best music and poetry in all literature had a like origin. It has been said that 'poets learn in suffering what they write in song.' Nothing really worthwhile comes without pain and cost. When we read some rich passage in Christian literature which just fits, we have no idea what it cost the writer in suffering to learn the truths set forth in those passages." Another has said that "sorrows come to stretch out spaces in the heart for joy.''

These are beautiful thoughts. It is true that even here and now, sorrow has its compensations. Many of these may be realized before the close of life's day. The discipline of sorrow pays rich dividends in the present. But those rewards are as the tip of an iceberg to the concealed portion when compared to the glory that shall be revealed. The primary purpose of sanctified affliction will not become apparent until the afterward when the Bride is on the throne. Then and only then will the meaning of Paul's glorious prophecy be revealed: ''Our light affliction, which is but for a moment, worketh for us a far more exceeding and eternal weight of glory.'' Do not try to fathom the effect and purpose of affliction now. Eternity alone will unveil its grandeur.

The Bride-elect — An Object Lesson in the Universe

We do not know the nature of God's eternal enterprise but we know that it is immeasurably great. ''Eye hath not seen, nor ear heard, neither have entered into the heart of man, the things which God hath prepared for them that love him'' (1 Cor. 2:9). We also know that the Church is the central factor, the chief personality, the ranking character, the stellar celebrity in that eternal kingdom. ''His intent was that now, *through the church*, the manifold wisdom of God should be made known to the rulers and authorities in the heavenly realms'' (Eph. 3:10 *NIV*).

What is the content of God's ''manifold wisdom'' which He is seeking to make known to the ''rulers and authorities in the heavenly realms'' *through the Church*? Since love is the law of the universe, and since the Church is in the school of suffering to learn love, that ''manifold wisdom'' must consist of a sublime dimension of agape love.

Because God plans to use the Church, the Bride-elect, in

eternity to express His love-nature to the principalities and powers, to all the intelligences of the universe, this is doubtless a principal reason He takes such pains to teach her individual members deep dimensions of agape love. There must be some things about God's love and the plan of salvation that are a mystery to the angels as suggested in 1 Peter 1:12, "Which things the angels desire to look into." Evidently God plans to use the Church to educate and enlighten the inhabitants of His ever-expanding celestial empire. HALLELUJAH!

The Centrality of the Church

"For by him all things were created: things in heaven and on earth, visible and invisible, whether thrones or [political] powers or rulers or authorities; all things were created by him and for him. He is before all things, and in him all things hold together. And he is the head of the body, the church" (Col. 1:16-18 *NIV*). This last statement is the clincher. It is reinforced by Ephesians 1:22, "And God placed all things under his feet and appointed him to be the head over everything *for the church*, which is his body, *the fullness of him* who fills everything in every way" (*NIV*). This last statement is another clincher. *He is head over everything FOR the Church*. All the divine enterprise revolves around the Church. Think of it! The Church is closer to the seat of universal power than all the vast array of current and future thrones, principalities, powers, rulers, and authorities in the universe (1 Cor. 3:21-23). In fact, the Church is so close to the seat of supreme authority that she is a part of it as His body and is to be enthroned with Him. Therefore, God will go to any length necessary to prepare the individual members for their exalted positions.

"The Worker Rather Than the Work"

This is why He will go to such pains to produce utter

brokenness, compassion, and agape love. For instance, sometimes God permits one of His servants a large measure of spiritual success for many years. He seems to bear a charmed life. Every effort he makes is prospered and blessed. Then God permits him to be overwhelmed with seeming disaster. He is utterly broken. A work of God, under his hand, perishes with apparent loss to the cause. It is a mystery. But God has a reason.

The Success of Failure

Sometimes, to suffer failure is the only way one can be decentralized. Sometimes the suffering of adversity, catastrophic disaster, and utter loss is necessary to produce the meekness, compassion, and selflessness without which one may remain unqualified for lofty eternal rank. Ill health may be followed by financial disaster, loss of reputation, or personal tragedies. If failure works better than success to prepare a man for rulership, you can be sure that God loves him too well to shield him at the expense of his "eternal weight of glory." God seems to endorse the theme, "The worker rather than the work," because God has eternal values in view. Oswald Chambers says: "Why shouldn't we go through heartbreaks? . . . If through a broken heart God can bring His purposes to pass in the world, then thank Him for breaking your heart."[2]

The Temporal Versus the Eternal

The temptation of many gifted religious leaders is to aim and work for temporal success, a kingdom of their own here and now. The present strong, almost exclusive emphasis upon the positive by some very successful religious entrepreneurs is an example.[3] The writer fears that some of these men will have to see their work shattered and broken by failure and defeat if they are to share that "eternal weight of glory" which Paul writes about. An unknown writer has voiced this viewpoint in the following lines:

While the voice of the world shouts its chorus,
  Its paean for those who have won;
While the trumpet is sounding triumphant,
  And high to the breeze and the sun,
Glad banners are waving, hands clapping,
  And hurrying feet thronging
After the laurel crowned victors,
  I stand on the field of defeat
In the shadow with those who are fallen and wounded
      and dying,
  And there chant a requiem low —
Place my hand on their pain-knitted brow,
  Breathe a prayer, hold a hand that is helpless,
And whisper, ''They only the victory win,
  Who have fought the good fight,
And have vanquished the demon that tempts us within.''

Mixed Motives

How many of us have mixed motives of which we are
totally unaware until God permits purifying adversity.
That ''demon within us'' is vain ambition, human energy,
and uncrucified flesh. God will go to any length to exorcise
it, even to the extent of allowing failure to an apparently
spiritual work. He is working for the man's eternal rank
and His own eternal glory. ''According to the grace of God
which is given unto me, as a wise master builder, I have
laid the foundation, and another buildeth on it. But let
every man take heed how he buildeth upon it. For other
foundation can no man lay than that which is laid, which is
Jesus Christ. Now if any man build upon this foundation
gold, silver, precious stones, wood, hay, stubble — every
man's work shall be made manifest; for the day shall
declare it, because it shall be revealed by fire; and the fire
shall test every man's work of what sort it is. If any man's

work abide which he hath built upon it, he shall receive a reward. If any man's work shall be burned, he shall suffer loss; but he himself shall be saved, yet as by fire" (1 Cor. 3:10-15 *New Scofield*).

The Worship of Success

This is a day when not only the secular world worships success, many church leaders are guilty as well. Success seems to be the god of some leaders of great ecclesiastical enterprises. John Henry Newman, who articulated this spiritual vice in the hymn "Lead, Kindly Light," has many brothers and sisters. He wrote:

> I loved the garish day in spite of fears,
>   Pride ruled my will,
> Remember not past years.

Only after a mighty breaking may some of us see our fault. It may take a lifetime for God to disillusion us with success, purify our motives, and mature us in agape love. It often seems that when some people have reached that maturity in love which renders them most effective, just when they have arrived at the peak of their usefulness here, God takes them to heaven. Many wonder why, when a person seems most ready for fruitful service, God summons him home. This makes no sense unless God's purpose in life is not primarily for service in time but for God's eternal enterprises. God has used the circumstances of life, whether of joy or sorrow, pleasure or pain, success or failure, to mature him for his exalted role in His future kingdom. When God has achieved this, there is little point in leaving him here longer.

To Live Life Over Again

Many times as a person nears the end of his days he becomes more conscious of eternal verities. In the light of passing years his perspective has changed. As the evening shadows lengthen, his system of values is revised. The things he once so highly prized now seem less important. The coveted goals of former years lose their fascination and charm. He has grown in wisdom. In retrospect he realizes his former folly and is tempted to wallow in vain regret. In this frame of mind, not realizing that life is made primarily for learning agape love, not for worldly success, one could wish that he might go back and live his life over again, using the wisdom that life has bestowed upon him. He may feel that, for him, life has been a monumental failure. *But from God's standpoint, if one has learned love, there would be no point in living life over again because the real purpose of life has been achieved.* "For life, with all it yields of joy or woe and hope and fear is just our chance o' the prize of learning love" (Browning).

Life Without Love a Disaster

The person who has made the most spectacular success but who reaches life's end without learning love has totally failed. Do not envy those in the limelight of publicity, those with scintillating intellects, or those who have accumulated great wealth and all that it affords. If one has not learned love in the process, his life is a disaster. Psalm 37 is very relevant here.

Life is for learning love, not for sensual pleasure, nor for accumulating riches, nor fame; not for building great manufacturing, commercial, or military empires, nor political power. It is not for exploration, travel, or conquest of outer space. It is not for learning science, history, economics, philosophy, or even theology; not for delivering great orations, preaching great sermons, or holding immense religious campaigns; not for the building of great institutions such as hospitals, churches, schools and colleges; nor for publishing books, magazines, or other periodicals. All of these are of value only as they grow out of or contribute to the learning or expression of love.

The Success of Learning Love

When one has learned love, he has succeeded in life no matter how he has failed otherwise. If all the failures in learning love in the past have at last produced this brokenness of spirit, that life has been no failure in God's sight because it was for this He was working. This is what God was after from the beginning, because agape love is essential for rulership in God's eternal social order. Indeed, love is the necessary ingredient for a truly successful life on earth — but its ultimate value is in qualifying one for eternal rulership in an economy where love is the supreme law.

The wreckage caused by the sorrow and grief intrinsic to a life of unlovingness is the price God is willing to pay to achieve brokenness, compassion, and tenderness of spirit. All sin is against love. *Success at the cost of love is failure. Winning at the cost of love is losing. LOVE NEVER FAILS.* "When the sun has grown old, and the stars have grown cold; when the oceans and rivers have run dry; when hoary time has passed away, when the solemn footsteps of eternity echo no more, love will still endure, all measureless and strong." It is the supreme law of the universe. It can never be broken with impunity.

ODE TO AGAPE LOVE
(With apologies to the Apostle Paul)

Though I become as rich as Croesus, King Midas, the Rockefellers, Howard Hughes, and Paul Getty combined, and have not LOVE, I am nothing.

Though I become as powerful as Nebuchadnezzar, Alexander the Great, Charlemagne, and Napoleon all together, and have not LOVE, I am nothing.

Though I have the eloquence of Demosthenes, Cicero, Shakespeare, Daniel Webster, and Churchill, so that I can sway multitudes, and have not LOVE, I am nothing.

Though I possess the beauty and charm of Helen of Troy, Cleopatra, and Miss Universe, and have not LOVE, I am nothing.

AGAPE LOVE NEVER FAILS!

Though there be wealth, it shall rust and decay.

Though there be fame, it shall sink into oblivion.

Though there be political power and supremacy, it shall burst like a bubble.

Though there be military might, it shall crumble.

Though there be tongues of eloquence, they shall be stilled.

Though there be beauty of face and form, it shall fade.

BUT LOVE IS FOREVER.

When hoary time shall be no more,
When earthly thrones and kingdoms fall,
When the Ancient of Days is set upon His Judgment Seat,
When angel harps are stilled and Heaven's silence fills the universe,
LOVE WILL STILL BE YOUNG.

When the last plane has made its flight,
The last satellite circled the globe,
The last rocket has been launched;
When the debris of the melting cosmos has been swept
afar by the fiery tempest of God's wrath;
When the new heaven and earth leap from the matrix
of the ages—
LOVE will still be in its infancy.
It will never grow old, never fade, never decay.
It is life's superlative goal.
It is divine.

Therefore, MAKE LOVE YOUR AIM!
—Anonymous

LIFE IS FOR LEARNING AGAPE LOVE.

NOTES

1. J. R. Miller, *The Ministry of Comfort*, p. 30.
2. Chambers, *My Utmost for His Highest*, p. 306. Used by permission.
3. See Billheimer, *Destined for the Throne*, "Ecclesiastical Treadmills," p. 101.

12

LEARNING AGAPE LOVE THROUGH AGING

Aging — A Part of God's Design

Previously it has been stated that all that befalls the obedient child of God is related to the development of character. Take for instance the process of aging. The world at large considers this as something to be evaded, avoided, and postponed as long as possible. All kinds of devices are employed to prolong the illusion of youth. It is usual to consider that aging is simply the natural consequence of the inexorable passing of time, to be greeted with nothing but regret. The youth cult would encourage the elderly to "think young," as though fancy could delay the inevitable flight of time. But aging is more than an unavoidable biological process. It has a purpose and is a part of God's design.

Aging and the Revision of Values

One of God's purposes in the process of aging is to enable one properly to revise his system of values. How different the priorities of youth and age. In youth one's goal is success, power, fame, rank, reputation, skill, wealth, and ease. Youth often believes that life is made primarily for pleasure. *Self* is the center. God intends that the vicissitudes of life, its disappointments, heartbreaks, and the infirmities of advancing years, shall change this. It is meant to disenchant one with earth and orient him heavenward. J. R. Miller says, "True living is really a succession of battles in which the better triumphs over the worse, the spirit over the flesh. Until we cease to live for self, we have not begun to live at all."[1]

"My Master"

An unknown author has eloquently and vividly described the transition from youth's vain ambitions to selfless devotion to the Master in the following stanzas:

I had walked life's path with an easy tread,
   Had followed where comforts and pleasures led,
Until one day, in a quiet place,
   I met my Master, face to face.

With station and rank and wealth for my goal,
   Much thought for my body — but none for my soul,
I had entered to win in life's mad race,
   When I met my Master, face to face.

I had built my castles and reared them high,
   Till their towers pierced the blue of the sky;
I had sworn to rule with an iron mace —
   When I met my Master, face to face.

I met Him, and knew Him, and blushed to see
   That His eyes full of sorrow were fixed on me;
And I faltered, and fell at His feet that day,
   While my castles melted and vanished away.

Melted and vanished, and in their place
   Naught else did I see but my Master's face;
And I cried aloud, "O make me meet
   To follow the steps of Thy wounded feet!"

My thought is now for the souls of men;
   I have lost my life to find it again,
E'er since that day, in a quiet place,
   I met my Master, face to face.

Purpose of the Passing Years

The purpose of the passing years, with their joys and sorrows, is to wean one from self-worship — to mature him in love. Getting older is not getting better unless it is delivering one from self-love. Growing older is intended to make one more gentle, more thoughtful and considerate, more gracious and sympathetic, less childish and demanding. This is the reason for the trials and tribulations, the conflicts with pain, the struggles with disease, the financial reverses, the ingratitude of loved ones, the disappointments of false friendships, wrongful suffering, and the grief of bereavement.

Aging — God's Finishing School

J. R. Miller says, ''Fruits are developed and ripened by the influence of weather and the climate. It takes all the different seasons, with their variety of climatic conditions, to bring fruit to maturity. Winter does its part as well as spring, summer, and autumn. Night and day, cloud and sunshine, cold and heat, wind and calm, all work together to ripen the fruit.'' [2]

In like manner, all life's varied experiences, even down to old age, are working together to mature and ripen *character* and develop agape love. All sunshine would not make good fruit, nor would all gladness and joy produce the richest character. Darkness as well as light, rough cold weather as well as gentle warm summer, are needed to mature and enrich character in agape love.

Aging, therefore, is not just something to be endured as an unfortunate but unavoidable evil. It is a part of God's plan. When properly accepted, it may constitute God's finishing school for character education and enrichment before entering eternity.

Wasting Retirement Years

Gerontologists are concerned that early retirement is an unnecessary waste of manpower. Nowhere is this more true than in the life of the aging believer. The great temptation following retirement is to follow the pattern of the world and do one's own pleasure. Upon retirement, those sufficiently affluent often decide that now is the time to satisfy their own desires and do the things they had always wanted to do. They often embark upon a program of travel, sightseeing, entertainment, and other forms of self-pleasing. Others, less affluent, may spend their time in frustration, bemoaning their fate, envying others, and languishing in self-pity. Believers indulging in these vices are *wasting their sorrows.*

Making Retirement Productive

God desires to utilize for the specific purpose of intercession the long period of physical decline which comes to many people. Spiritually, this can be the most productive period of life. In *Destined for the Throne* it is shown that "prayer is where the action is," that "the most important thing anyone can do for God or man is to pray"; that "you can do more than pray *after* you have prayed but you cannot do more than pray *until* you have prayed"; that "the Church, through believing prayer, holds the balance of power both in world affairs and in the salvation of individual souls"; and that "the fate of the world is in the hands of nameless saints."

Satanic Strategy

Since this is true, elderly and retired people could and should be the greatest force available to God in influencing world affairs and the salvation of souls. During active life it is more difficult to find sufficient time to pray. Pastors, evangelists, administrators, and other Christian workers are in the same dilemma. Unless they have been well taught concerning the importance of prayer and the devotional life they are in grave danger of relegating it to a place of secondary importance. Satan's most successful strategy is to keep Christian workers so busy in secondary things that they have little time for the primary thing — *prayer.* Thus the "good" becomes the enemy of the "best."

All of the most heinous forms of evil in the world are the result of demon activity. The only power that controls them is the power of the Holy Spirit. And the Holy Spirit, by His own choice, is released to do His work only by the prayers of holy ˙people (Matt. 16:18-19 and John 20:21-23).[3] This is why John Wesley said, "God will do nothing but in answer to prayer."

Priority of Prayer

> *From heaven's standpoint, all spiritual victories are won, not primarily in the pulpit, not primarily in the klieg lights of publicity, nor yet through the ostentatious blaring of trumpets, but in the secret place of prayer. . . .*
> Thank God for the gifts, talents, and preaching ability of men like Billy Graham. This is no effort to depreciate these assets. But the power that has transformed multiplied thousands through Billy Graham's ministry is not the power of superior gifts, unusual talents, brilliant rhetoric, or psychological persuasiveness, but the power released by the prayer and faith of the millions of his prayer helpers. From heaven's standpoint, the combined prayer and intercession which surrounds and supports Billy Graham is the real explanation of what is taking place. Because of the immense program of prayer warfare on his behalf, Satan's legions opposing his efforts are overcome and bound in the same way

they were when Moses, Aaron, and Hur interceded for Joshua and Israel against Amalek. [4]

Prayer Is Where the Action Is

Many people grieve because they have been denied service on the mission field or in some other chosen endeavor. *Through faithful intercession they may accomplish as much and reap as full a reward as though they had been on the field in person.* Those who lament that they have been cheated in life because they have no shining gifts or spectacular talents, or those who have been retired by age or illness, may, through faithful intercession, share in the heavenly reward equally with the most highly endowed, all because PRAYER IS WHERE THE ACTION IS. "He that receiveth a prophet in the name of a prophet shall receive a prophet's reward; and he that receiveth a righteous man in the name of a righteous man shall receive a righteous man's reward" (Matt. 10:41). If simple hospitality brings equal compensation, then a prayer support ministry will surely not go unrewarded. [5]

Prayer Warfare Is Running Interference

There is only one Billy Graham. There will never be another. But, according to the principle articulated by Jesus in the above-quoted scripture, the lowliest saint who faithfully labors in prayer on Billy's behalf will as surely share in his reward as if he personally possessed all the gifts with which God has endowed the famous evangelist.

This same principle applies in the work of any and every spiritual leader. To the extent that one is faithful in prayer warfare on behalf of those God has placed in positions of responsibility and leadership in soul-winning and kingdom affairs, such as missionaries, pastors, evangelists, teachers, administrators — to that extent he will share in the eternal reward which will be meted out to these workers in that day. To use an athletic metaphor: prayer warfare is running interference for the one who is carrying the ball.

The Fate of the World

This leaves no room for self-pity or envy of those more gifted, provided one is willing to fill his place as a prayer warrior. *In heaven's "book" the nameless saint in the most remote and secluded spot, completely lost to view, and overshadowed in the battle, is just as important, and if he is faithful, will receive just as great a reward, as the most heralded and gifted leader. Hallelujah!* All of the faithful prayer warriors are just as truly at the front and are making just as great a contribution in the fray as the apparent leader. And they will share equally in the reward. Verily, "The fate of the world is in the hands of nameless saints." [6]

A Viable Alternative

Since these things are true, then no believer needs ever to retire and no period of life needs to be unproductive. By means of intercession, he can be as truly in the front line in a wheelchair or an invalid's bed as those who are active. It requires and develops more character to pray than to preach, sing, or organize city-wide campaigns. There are enough elderly believers (many of whom feel they are laid on the shelf as useless) who, if they could see that prayer is the most important thing anyone can do for God or man, and would be willing to discipline themselves to a life of prayer — there are enough of them to turn this nation around; *and praying saints are the only ones who can!* "The righteous shall flourish like the palm tree: . . They shall still bring forth fruit in old age" (Psalm 92:12,14). It is sad that any elderly believer should waste what could be his most productive years in self-pleasing or self-pity.

The following lines suggest a viable alternative:

> I cannot go on — I wonder why!
> Is my life spent, will I soon die?
> If I could have another life to live —
> But no! He only gives us one in which
> To gain or lose a crown.
>
> O come, my soul! Thou still dost live;
> Why languish longer? Arise and give
> Thy best to the task. The night comes on.
> Thou art not too old — who said you were?
> God sets no age — not in His Word,
> Though Satan in his subtle way
> Has set you back, no longer stay.
>
> Arise! And give what you have left
> To make Christ known to souls bereft.
> His hand leads on, pray follow fast,
> The time grows short, then heav'n at last. [7]
>
> —Alvin A. Rasmussen

Remember, you are destined for the throne! God is training you now. Your trials are not an accident: no suffering is purposeless. Your eternal profit is in view. Therefore, *don't waste your sorrows!*

NOTES

1. J. R. Miller, *Making the Most of Life*, p. 2.
2. Miller, *The Upper Currents*, p. 94.
3. See Billheimer, *Destined for the Throne*, pp. 43-51.
4. *Ibid.*, pp. 104-105.
5. *Ibid.*, pp. 105-106.
6. *Ibid.*, p. 106.
7. Alvin A. Rasmussen, "You're Not Too Old," 1952, first published in *Brown Gold,* magazine of New Tribes Mission, Woodworth, Wis. Adapted. Used by permission of the author.